Better Homes and Gardens®

Pancakes

& Toppings

By Darlene Kronschnabel

Better Homes and Gardens® Books
Des Moines, Iowa

Better Homes and Gardens® Books
An imprint of Meredith® Books

Pancakes & Toppings
Author: Darlene Kronschnabel
Editor: Jennifer Darling
Contributing Editor: Linda J. Henry
Associate Art Director: Tom Wegner
Copy Chief: Angela K. Renkoski
Copy Editor: Jennifer Speer Ramundt
Test Kitchen Director: Sharon Stilwell
Test Kitchen Product Supervisor: Dianna Nolin
Photographer: Mike Dieter
Food Stylists: Jennifer Peterson, Janet Pittman
Editorial and Design Assistants: Judy Bailey, Paula Forest, Jennifer Norris, Karen Schirm
Production Manager: Douglas M. Johnston
Prepress Coordinator: Marjorie J. Schenkelberg

Editor in Chief: James D. Blume
Vice President, Retail Sales: Jamie L. Martin
Director, New Product Development: Ray Wolf
Managing Editor: Christopher Cavanaugh

Better Homes and Gardens® Magazine
Editor in Chief: Jean LemMon
Executive Food Editor: Nancy Byal

Meredith Publishing Group
President, Publishing Group: Christopher M. Little
Vice President and Publishing Director: John P. Loughlin

Meredith Corporation
Chairman and Chief Executive Officer: Jack D. Rehm
President and Chief Operating Officer: William T. Kerr
Chairman of the Executive Committee: E.T. Meredith III

Cover photo: Basic Buttermilk Pancakes (page 7)

Some of the images in this book are used by permission of Zedcor, Inc., Tucson, Arizona, from the 100,000-image DeskGallery® collection; 800/482-4567.

All of us at Better Homes and Gardens® Books are dedicated to providing you with the information and ideas you need to create delicious foods. We welcome your comments and suggestions. Write to us at: Better Homes and Gardens® Books, Cookbook Editorial Department, RW-240, 1716 Locust St., Des Moines, IA 50309–3023.

Our seal assures you that every recipe in *Pancakes & Toppings* has been tested in the Better Homes and Gardens® Test Kitchen. This means that each recipe is practical and reliable, and meets our high standards of taste appeal. We guarantee your satisfaction with this book for as long as you own it.

Contents

Introduction 4

Making the Perfect Pancake 5

American Classics 7

International Pancakes 16

Fruit Pancakes 26

Vegetable Pancakes 36

Savory Specialties 48

Dessert Pancakes 62

Kid-Pleasing Pancakes 71

Pancake Mixes 80

Toppings 94

Index 110

Metric Conversions 112

Introduction

I don't recall the exact moment I connected with pancakes. It most certainly happened, though, in my Hungarian mother's kitchen, where she made sour milk pancakes so often that I took them for granted. They were tender, thin, light, and topped with melted butter and syrup for breakfast. If any were left over, Mother spread them with jam and rolled them jelly-roll fashion for mid-morning snacks. She even put them in our school lunch buckets.

Later, thanks to my father's parents, I realized that there was more to pancakes than my mother's variety. My grandparents lived in northern Wisconsin, where hunters by the dozens turned up at their deer-hunting camp to enjoy Minnie Doughty's famous sourdough buckwheat pancakes. With my grandmother at one stove and me at another, we baked hundreds of pancakes and poured steaming mugs of coffee for hunters at the crack of dawn. In later years, when I asked for her sourdough buckwheat pancake recipe, Grandma just laughed. She eventually sent me a recipe she found in a farm paper, though, claiming it was as close as she could come to a family-size recipe. That was the start of my pancake recipe collection.

—Darlene Kronschnabel

Darlene Kronschnabel—former Wisconsin innkeeper and nationally syndicated food columnist, and author of Better Homes and Gardens® Pancakes and Toppings—has been collecting pancake recipes for years. As her recipe collection

has grown, pancakes have become more than a breakfast standard at her house, playing a starring role in lunch, dinner, and dessert.

This collection, all tested and approved by the Better Homes and Gardens® Test Kitchen, highlights dinner and dessert recipes as well as traditional breakfast ideas. If you need a quick meal solution, the chapter on pancake mixes will put you a step ahead. And you'll find plenty of scrumptious homemade syrups, sauces, and butters to top off your pancake selection.

What is it about pancakes that sparks true devotion? Perhaps it's their easy-going nature, their simplicity, or their versatility. The exact answer remains a mystery. But according to Darlene, one thing's for sure: Once you savor their goodness, you remain a fan for life.

Making the Perfect Pancake

Besides being excellent light meal fare, pancakes are easy to prepare and require no tricky techniques. A few pointers will ensure success.

Mixing the Batter

Begin by combining all of the dry ingredients in a mixing bowl and stirring them together until they're well combined. Beat the whole eggs or egg yolks (if they're included) in another mixing bowl, one that's large enough to also hold the liquid ingredients. If the recipe calls for beating egg whites, see the tip on page 36.

Stir the liquid ingredients quickly into the dry ingredients. To make your pancakes light and tender, stir the batter just until the ingredients are combined but still slightly lumpy.

Any small lumps left in the batter will cook out on the griddle, and overmixing destroys the air bubbles in the batter, resulting in heavy, tough pancakes.

Griddles

One of the secrets to producing great pancakes is to use a griddle or heavy skillet that heats evenly. Look for one with a cooking surface that is large enough to cook several pancakes at one time.

Our recipes call for cooking pancakes on a lightly greased griddle or skillet. An easy way to do this is to put a small amount of shortening on a piece of waxed paper or a pastry brush and rub or brush across the griddle or skillet surface before heating. Or, give the cold pan a quick spray with nonstick spray coating. If your griddle or skillet has a nonstick surface, it may not be necessary to grease the surface.

Cooking

Wait until your griddle is heated to medium heat (or whatever other temperature the recipe directs) before pouring the pancake batter on it. Test the griddle by dripping a few drops of water on it. If the water dances over the surface, the griddle is ready.

For a nice round pancake, pour your batter on the griddle from a measuring cup, a pitcher, or a small gravy ladle with a spout that will give an even flow. Whatever you use, hold it close to the griddle surface and pour into a pool that will spread out into an even shape. Don't crowd your griddle—the pancakes will cook better and look better if they don't run together.

As your pancakes are cooking, keep an eye on the griddle temperature. You may need to adjust the heat to get satisfactory results. The more pancakes you make, the easier it will become to determine the ideal temperature.

The pancakes are ready to turn when the undersides are golden brown and the top surfaces are evenly covered with tiny, unbroken bubbles. Use the edge of a spatula (a round one of good size is helpful) to carefully check if the undersides are browned. If the pancakes are too brown on the bottoms before bubbles form on the tops, your griddle is too hot. If the tops bake dry before the bottoms are browned, the griddle is too cool. Adjust the heat accordingly.

When the pancakes are golden brown on both sides, remove them from the griddle—and enjoy!

Basic Buttermilk Pancakes

Besides being delicious, these classic pancakes (pictured on the cover) are quick to fix, making them a wonderful Sunday morning recipe.

Prep: 15 minutes
Makes 20 pancakes

2½ **cups all-purpose flour**
  2 **tablespoons sugar**
  1 **teaspoon baking powder**
  1 **teaspoon baking soda**
 ½ **teaspoon salt**
  2 **eggs, slightly beaten**
2½ **cups buttermilk**
  2 **tablespoons margarine or butter, melted**
  1 **teaspoon vanilla**

1. In a mixing bowl combine flour, sugar, baking powder, baking soda, and salt. In another mixing bowl combine eggs, buttermilk, margarine or butter, and vanilla. Add to flour mixture. Stir just until combined but still slightly lumpy.

2. Heat a lightly greased griddle or heavy skillet over medium heat until a few drops of water dance across the surface. For each pancake, pour about ¼ cup batter onto the hot griddle. Spread batter into a circle about 4 inches in diameter.

3. Cook over medium heat until pancakes are golden brown, turning to cook second sides when pancake surfaces are bubbly and edges are slightly dry (about 2 to 3 minutes per side). Serve immediately or keep warm in a loosely covered ovenproof dish in a 300° oven. Makes 20 pancakes.

Nutrition Facts per pancake: 88 calories, 2 g total fat (1 g saturated fat), 22 mg cholesterol, 187 mg sodium, 14 g carbohydrates, 0 g fiber, 3 g protein **Daily Values:** 2% vit. A, 0% vit. C, 4% calcium, 5% iron

Blueberry Buttermilk Pancakes: Prepare as above, except sprinkle 1 to 2 tablespoons *fresh or frozen blueberries* on the pancakes before turning to cook second sides.
Cheese Buttermilk Pancakes: Prepare as above, except omit vanilla and stir ½ cup shredded *cheddar cheese* into batter. If desired, serve with additional cheddar cheese.

Keep 'Em Hot

Piping hot— that's when pancakes are at their best. So keep the first ones warm while you finish cooking the remaining batches. Place the pancakes hot from the griddle in an ovenproof container or on a baking sheet in a 300° oven. Loosely cover them with aluminum foil.

Pumpkin Pancakes

Prep: 20 minutes
Makes 16 pancakes

2 cups all-purpose flour
2 tablespoons brown sugar
1 tablespoon baking powder
$\frac{1}{2}$ teaspoon salt
$\frac{1}{2}$ teaspoon ground cinnamon
$\frac{1}{4}$ teaspoon baking soda
$\frac{1}{4}$ teaspoon ground nutmeg
$\frac{1}{4}$ teaspoon ground ginger
$1\frac{1}{2}$ cups milk
1 cup canned pumpkin or mashed, cooked pumpkin
2 egg yolks
3 tablespoons margarine or butter, melted
1 teaspoon finely shredded orange peel (optional)
2 egg whites
$\frac{1}{3}$ cup chopped pecans (optional)
1 recipe Cider and Maple Syrup (see page 95) (optional)

1. In a mixing bowl combine flour, brown sugar, baking powder, salt, cinnamon, baking soda, nutmeg, and ginger. In another mixing bowl combine milk, pumpkin, egg yolks, margarine, and, if desired, orange peel. Add pumpkin mixture to flour mixture. Stir just until combined but still slightly lumpy.

2. In a medium mixing bowl beat egg whites until stiff peaks form (tips stand straight). Gently fold beaten egg whites into batter, leaving a few puffs of white. Do not overbeat.

3. Heat a lightly greased griddle or heavy skillet over medium heat until a few drops of water dance across the surface. For each pancake, pour about $\frac{1}{4}$ cup batter onto the hot griddle. Spread batter into a circle about 4 inches in diameter.

4. Cook over medium heat until pancakes are golden brown, turning to cook second sides when pancake surfaces are bubbly and edges are slightly dry (about 1 to 2 minutes per side). If desired, sprinkle about 1 teaspoon chopped pecans on pancakes before turning to cook second sides. Serve immediately or keep warm in a loosely covered ovenproof dish in a 300° oven. If desired, serve with Cider and Maple Syrup. Makes 16 pancakes.

Nutrition Facts per pancake: 104 calories, 3 g total fat (1 g saturated fat), 28 mg cholesterol, 200 mg sodium, 15 g carbohydrates, 1 g fiber, 3 g protein
Daily Values: 41% vit. A, 1% vit. C, 8% calcium, 7% iron

Pumpkin Pancakes with Cider and Maple Syrup

Whole Wheat Griddle Cakes

Prep: 15 minutes
Makes 16 pancakes

*The hearty whole wheat flavor comes not only from the whole wheat flour,
but from the wheat germ as well.*

Pancake Lore

The name pancake didn't become common until the late 1800s. Before that, they were called flapjacks, buckwheat cakes, griddle cakes, hotcakes, flannel cakes, hoecakes, or slapjacks.

1½ cups whole wheat flour
½ cup toasted wheat germ
2 tablespoons brown sugar
1 teaspoon baking powder
½ teaspoon baking soda
¼ teaspoon salt
2 eggs, slightly beaten
2 cups buttermilk
2 tablespoons margarine or
   butter, melted
1 teaspoon vanilla
   Milk (optional)

1. In a mixing bowl combine whole wheat flour, wheat germ, brown sugar, baking powder, baking soda, and salt. In another mixing bowl combine eggs, buttermilk, margarine or butter, and vanilla. Add to the flour mixture. Stir just until combined but still slightly lumpy. (Batter will thicken on standing. For a thinner consistency, add milk, 1 tablespoon at a time, until the desired consistency is reached.)

2. Heat a lightly greased griddle or heavy skillet over medium heat until a few drops of water dance across the surface. For each pancake, pour about ¼ cup batter onto the hot griddle. Spread batter into a circle about 4 inches in diameter.

3. Cook over medium heat until pancakes are golden brown, turning to cook second sides when pancake surfaces are bubbly and edges are slightly dry (about 1 to 2 minutes per side). Serve immediately or keep warm in a loosely covered ovenproof dish in a 300° oven. Makes 16 pancakes.

Nutrition Facts per pancake: 92 calories, 3 g total fat (1 g saturated fat),
28 mg cholesterol, 153 mg sodium, 13 g carbohydrates, 1 g fiber, 4 g protein
Daily Values: 3% vit. A, 0% vit. C, 5% calcium, 6% iron

Honey-Oatmeal Pancakes

Make a tasty variation of these tender, light pancakes by adding ½ teaspoon ground cinnamon to the flour mixture. Then fold 1 cup finely chopped, peeled apple into the batter.

Prep: 15 minutes
Stand: 10 minutes
Makes 12 pancakes

½ cup whole wheat flour
1 tablespoon brown sugar
1 teaspoon baking powder
½ teaspoon salt
1¼ cups quick-cooking
    rolled oats
1¼ cups milk
2 eggs, slightly beaten
3 tablespoons margarine or
    butter, melted
2 tablespoons honey
   Milk (optional)

1. In a large mixing bowl combine whole wheat flour, brown sugar, baking powder, and salt. In another mixing bowl combine rolled oats and milk; let stand 10 minutes. Add the eggs, margarine or butter, and honey to the oat mixture. Beat until well combined. Add the oat mixture to the flour mixture. Stir just until combined but still slightly lumpy. (If batter is too thick, thin by adding milk, 1 tablespoon at a time, until desired consistency is reached.)

2. Heat a lightly greased griddle or heavy skillet over medium heat until a few drops of water dance across the surface. For each pancake, pour about ¼ cup batter onto the hot griddle. Spread batter into a circle about 4 inches in diameter.

3. Cook over medium heat until pancakes are golden brown, turning to cook the second sides when pancake surfaces are bubbly and edges are slightly dry (about 1 to 2 minutes per side). Serve immediately or keep warm in a loosely covered ovenproof dish in a 300° oven. Makes 12 pancakes.

Nutrition Facts per pancake: 114 calories, 5 g total fat (1 g saturated fat), 37 mg cholesterol, 177 mg sodium, 14 g carbohydrates, 1 g fiber, 4 g protein
Daily Values: 6% vit. A, 0% vit. C, 6% calcium, 5% iron

Raisin-Honey-Oatmeal Pancakes: Prepare as above, except cover ½ cup *raisins* with hot water. Let stand 15 minutes. Drain; add raisins to batter. (Or, soak raisins in 3 tablespoons *rum*. Let stand 15 minutes. Do not drain; add raisin mixture to batter.)

Gingerbread Pancakes with Lemon Sauce

Gingerbread Pancakes

For breakfast or brunch, serve these molasses and spice pancakes with poached apple slices and crisp bacon strips.

Prep: 15 minutes

Makes 16 pancakes

2 cups all-purpose flour
1 teaspoon ground cinnamon
1 teaspoon ground ginger
1 teaspoon ground nutmeg
¾ teaspoon baking powder
¾ teaspoon baking soda
¼ teaspoon salt
2 eggs, slightly beaten
1¼ cups buttermilk
⅓ cup molasses
⅓ cup strong coffee
3 tablespoons cooking oil
1 recipe Lemon Sauce
    (see page 106) or 1 recipe
    Brandied Lemon Butter
    (see page 104) (optional)

1. In a mixing bowl combine flour, cinnamon, ginger, nutmeg, baking powder, baking soda, and salt. In another mixing bowl combine eggs, buttermilk, molasses, coffee, and oil. Add to flour mixture. Stir just until combined but still slightly lumpy.

2. Heat a lightly greased griddle or heavy skillet over medium heat until a few drops of water dance across the surface. For each pancake, pour about ¼ cup batter onto the hot griddle. Spread batter into a circle about 4 inches in diameter.

3. Cook over medium heat until pancakes are golden brown, turning to cook second sides when pancake surfaces are bubbly and edges are slightly dry (about 1 to 2 minutes per side). Serve immediately or keep warm in a loosely covered ovenproof dish in a 300° oven. If desired, serve with Lemon Sauce or Brandied Lemon Butter. Makes 16 pancakes.

Nutrition Facts per pancake: 110 calories, 4 g total fat (1 g saturated fat), 27 mg cholesterol, 139 mg sodium, 17 g carbohydrates, 0 g fiber, 3 g protein
Daily Values: 1% vit. A, 0% vit. C, 4% calcium, 7% iron

Sourdough Pancakes

Since colonial days, Americans have been saving a portion of the "soured" dough from one batch of bread to leaven the next. Westward pioneers used sourdough in loaves, flapjacks, and biscuits.

Sourdough Starter
- 1 package active dry yeast
- 2½ cups warm water (105° to 115°)
- 2 cups all-purpose flour
- 1 tablespoon sugar or honey

Pancakes
- 1¼ cups Sourdough Starter
- 1 cup all-purpose flour
- 1 tablespoon sugar
- 1 teaspoon baking powder
- ½ teaspoon baking soda
- ¼ teaspoon salt
- 1 egg, slightly beaten
- 2 tablespoons cooking oil

To Replenish Sourdough Starter

For every 1 cup of starter used, stir ¾ cup all-purpose flour, ¾ cup water, and 1 teaspoon sugar or honey into the remaining amount. Cover the starter and let stand at room temperature at least 1 day or until it's bubbly; refrigerate for later use.

1. For sourdough starter, dissolve yeast in ½ cup of the warm water. Add remaining warm water, flour, and sugar or honey, stirring until smooth. Cover with 100-percent-cotton cheesecloth. Let stand at room temperature (75° to 85°) for 5 to 10 days or until mixture has a sour, fermented aroma, stirring 2 or 3 times each day. (Fermentation time depends upon the room temperature; a warmer room hastens fermentation.) When starter is fermented, transfer to a 1-quart jar. Cover with cheesecloth; refrigerate. Do not cover with a tight-fitting lid. If starter isn't used within 10 days, stir in 1 teaspoon *sugar or honey*. Repeat every 10 days until some of the starter is used (see tip, left).

2. For pancakes, bring starter to room temperature. Mix flour, sugar, baking powder, baking soda, and salt. Mix egg, starter, and oil. Add to flour mixture. Stir until combined but still slightly lumpy. Heat a lightly greased griddle or heavy skillet over medium heat until a few drops of water dance across the surface. For each pancake, pour about ¼ cup batter onto hot griddle. Spread batter into a circle about 4 inches in diameter. Cook over medium heat until pancakes are golden brown, turning to cook second sides when surfaces are bubbly and edges are slightly dry (1 to 2 minutes per side). Serve immediately or keep warm in a loosely covered ovenproof dish in a 300° oven. Makes 10 pancakes.

Nutrition Facts per pancake: 124 calories, 4 g total fat (1 g saturated fat), 21 mg cholesterol, 160 mg sodium, 20 g carbohydrates, 1 g fiber, 3 g protein
Daily Values: 0% vit. A, 0% vit. C, 3% calcium, 8% iron

Wheat Cake Wrap-Ups

Try these buckwheat pancakes wrapped around sausage links for breakfast, brunch, or even a late evening snack.

Prep: 20 minutes
Makes 10 wrap-ups

1 8-ounce package fully cooked heat-and-serve turkey sausage links (10 links)
1 cup buttermilk
1 egg yolk
2 tablespoons margarine or butter, melted
1 cup Buckwheat Pancake Mix (see page 89)
1 egg white
  Milk (optional)
1 recipe Apricot Topping (see page 108) (optional)

1. Cook sausage links according to package directions; keep warm. Meanwhile, in a medium mixing bowl combine buttermilk, egg yolk, and margarine or butter. Add to Buckwheat Pancake Mix. Stir just until combined but still slightly lumpy.

2. In a small mixing bowl beat egg white with an electric mixer on medium to high speed until stiff peaks form (tips stand straight up). Gently fold beaten egg white into batter, leaving a few puffs of egg white. Do not overbeat.

3. Heat a lightly greased griddle or heavy skillet over medium heat until a few drops of water dance across the surface. For each pancake, pour about ¼ cup batter onto the hot griddle. Spread batter into a circle about 4 inches in diameter. (Pancakes need to be thin enough to roll easily. If batter is too thick to spread out properly, add milk, 1 tablespoon at a time, until desired consistency is reached.)

4. Cook over medium heat until pancakes are golden brown, turning to cook second sides when pancake surfaces are bubbly and edges are slightly dry (about 1 to 2 minutes per side). As soon as pancakes are removed from the griddle, roll each one around a cooked sausage link. Keep warm in a loosely covered ovenproof dish in a 300° oven. If desired, serve with Apricot Topping. Makes 10 pancake wrap-ups.

Nutrition Facts per wrap-up: 114 calories, 5 g total fat (1 g saturated fat), 37 mg cholesterol, 415 mg sodium, 11 g carbohydrates, 2 g fiber, 7 g protein
Daily Values: 6% vit. A, 0% vit. C, 6% calcium, 6% iron

Apfelpfannkuchen

(German Apple Pancake)
*You also can bake this puffy German pancake in a 9-inch pie plate,
as we did for the photo on page 17.*

Prep: 10 minutes
Bake: 18 minutes
Oven: 450°
Makes 6 servings

Pancake

3 eggs
½ cup all-purpose flour
½ cup milk
2 tablespoons margarine or
    butter, melted
¼ teaspoon salt

Filling

2 tablespoons margarine
    or butter
⅓ cup packed brown sugar
2 medium cooking apples,
    peeled, cored, and thinly
    sliced (2 cups)
¼ teaspoon ground cinnamon
¼ teaspoon ground nutmeg

Sifted powdered sugar

1. In a medium mixing bowl beat eggs with a wire whisk until frothy. Add flour, milk, *1 tablespoon* of the melted margarine or butter, and salt; beat until smooth.

2. Heat an 8-inch round baking pan or ovenproof skillet in a 450° oven for 2 minutes. Add remaining 1 tablespoon melted margarine; swirl to coat pan. Pour batter into hot pan. Bake pancake in the 450° oven for 18 to 20 minutes or until puffed and golden.

3. Meanwhile, for filling, in a medium skillet melt the 2 tablespoons margarine or butter over medium heat. Stir in brown sugar until combined. Stir in apple slices, cinnamon, and nutmeg. Cook, uncovered, for 3 to 5 minutes or until apples are crisp-tender, stirring occasionally.

4. To serve, remove pancake from oven. Spoon some of the filling into center of pancake. Sprinkle with powdered sugar. Cut into wedges. Pass the remaining filling. Pancake will collapse as it cools. Makes 6 servings.

Nutrition Facts per serving: 217 calories, 11 g total fat (3 g saturated fat), 108 mg cholesterol, 223 mg sodium, 26 g carbohydrates, 1 g fiber, 5 g protein
Daily Values: 15% vit. A, 3% vit. C, 4% calcium, 7% iron

Apfelpfannkuchen (German Apple Pancake)

Palatchinken

Prep: 10 minutes
Makes 8 pancakes

(Austrian Pancakes)
These quick, easy pancakes could prove a delicious addition to your list of simple,
light lunches for children of all ages.

Toasting Nuts

*T*oasting nuts not only brings out their flavor, but also keeps them crisp when they're used in sauces or other moist mixtures. To toast nuts, place them in a shallow baking pan. Bake in a 350° oven for 5 to 10 minutes or until they start to brown, stirring once or twice. To save time later, toast more than you need and freeze the extras in an airtight container.

¾ cup apricot preserves or
    plum jam
⅓ cup ground toasted walnuts
3 eggs
1½ cups milk
¼ cup margarine or butter,
    melted
1½ cups all-purpose flour
2 tablespoons granulated sugar
¼ teaspoon salt
2 tablespoons powdered sugar

1. In a small mixing bowl combine preserves or jam and walnuts; set aside.

2. In a large mixing bowl beat eggs, milk, and margarine or butter with an electric mixer on medium to high speed until well combined. Add flour, granulated sugar, and salt; beat until smooth.

3. Heat a lightly greased, large, nonstick skillet with flared sides over medium heat until a few drops of water dance across the surface. For each pancake, pour about ⅓ cup batter into the hot skillet. Quickly lift and tilt skillet to spread the batter into an even 8-inch circle. Cook over medium heat for 1½ to 2 minutes or until batter appears firm and undersides are lightly browned. Invert pancake onto an ovenproof plate. Keep warm in a loosely covered ovenproof dish in a 300° oven.

4. To serve, spread the unbrowned side of each pancake with a rounded tablespoon of the walnut mixture. Roll up jelly-roll style. If desired, cut in half. Sprinkle pancakes with powdered sugar. Makes 8 pancakes.

Nutrition Facts per pancake: 312 calories, 12 g total fat (3 g saturated fat), 83 mg cholesterol, 185 mg sodium, 46 g carbohydrates, 1 g fiber, 7 g protein
Daily Values: 13% vit. A, 2% vit. C, 6% calcium, 11% iron

Plättar

(Swedish Pancakes)

When baked properly, plättar should turn out looking as pretty as little lace doilies. Traditionally, these Swedish pancakes are baked in special cast-iron griddles that have seven 2½-inch-wide depressions for individual pancakes. However, any skillet can be used.

Prep: 10 minutes
Makes 40 pancakes

¾ cup all-purpose flour
2 tablespoons sugar
¼ teaspoon salt
1 egg
1 egg yolk
1 cup milk
1 tablespoon margarine or
   butter, melted
½ teaspoon vanilla
1 tablespoon cooking oil
   Lingonberry preserves or
   whole cranberry sauce
   (optional)

1. In a mixing bowl combine flour, sugar, and salt. In another mixing bowl beat egg and egg yolk with an electric mixer on medium to high speed for 3 to 5 minutes or until thick and lemon-colored. Add milk, margarine or butter, and vanilla; beat until well combined. Add the flour mixture and beat until smooth (batter will be thin).

2. Use a pastry brush to lightly coat a 12-inch skillet with oil (brush skillet with additional oil as needed). Heat over medium heat until a few drops of water dance across the surface. For each pancake, pour about 1 tablespoon batter into the hot skillet. Spread batter into a circle about 3 inches in diameter. (Or, use a 6- or 8-inch skillet with flared sides and 2 tablespoons batter per pancake; lift and tilt the skillet to make pancakes that are about 6 inches in diameter.)

3. Cook over medium heat about 1 minute or until undersides are golden brown. Loosen edges with a small spatula. Turn pancakes and cook about 1 minute more or until second sides are golden brown. If desired, serve with lingonberry preserves or whole cranberry sauce. Makes forty 3-inch pancakes or twenty 6-inch pancakes.

Nutrition Facts per 3-inch pancake: 22 calories, 1 g total fat (0 g saturated fat), 11 mg cholesterol, 22 mg sodium, 3 g carbohydrates, 0 g fiber, 1 g protein
Daily Values: 1% vit. A, 0% vit. C, 0% calcium, 0% iron

Sweet Hungarian Palacsinta

Sweet Hungarian Palacsinta

Handle these thin dessert pancakes carefully—they are quite delicate.

Prep: 25 minutes
Bake: 10 minutes
Oven: 300°
Makes 4 servings

½ cup sugar
¼ cup ground walnuts
1 teaspoon ground cinnamon
¼ cup margarine or butter, softened
¼ teaspoon salt
5 egg yolks
¾ cup all-purpose flour
½ cup milk
½ teaspoon vanilla
5 egg whites

1. Combine ¼ *cup* of the sugar, the walnuts, and cinnamon; set aside. Combine the remaining ¼ cup sugar, the margarine or butter, and salt. Beat with an electric mixer on medium speed until thoroughly combined. Add eggs yolks; beat well. Beat in flour. Add milk and vanilla; beat until well combined. Wash beaters thoroughly; beat egg whites with an electric mixer on medium to high speed until soft peaks form (tips curl). Fold egg whites into batter, leaving a few puffs of egg white. Do not overbeat.

2. Heat a lightly greased griddle or heavy skillet over medium heat until a few drops of water dance across surface. Reduce heat to medium-low. For each pancake, pour a scant ¼ cup batter onto hot griddle. Spread batter into a circle about 4 inches in diameter and ¼ inch thick. Cook over medium-low heat until pancakes are golden brown, turning to cook second sides when pancake surfaces are bubbly and edges are slightly dry (about 2 to 3 minutes per side). Repeat with remaining batter, making 16 pancakes.

3. Carefully transfer 4 pancakes to a foil-lined baking sheet. Sprinkle about 1½ teaspoons of the walnut mixture onto each pancake. Place a second pancake atop each first pancake and sprinkle with more nut mixture. Repeat stacking to make a total of 4 stacks of 4 pancakes each. Heat pancakes in a 300° oven about 10 minutes or until heated through. To serve, cut into pie-shaped wedges. Makes 4 servings.

Nutrition Facts per serving: 439 calories, 23 g total fat (5 g saturated fat), 269 mg cholesterol, 362 mg sodium, 46 g carbohydrates, 1 g fiber, 12 g protein
Daily Values: 56% vit. A, 1% vit. C, 7% calcium, 14% iron

Danish Aebleskiver

Prep: 15 minutes
Makes 30 aebleskiver

*Aebleskiver are cooked in a special 7-cup pan found in gourmet cookware shops.
When cooking these round pancakes, keep in mind that practice makes perfect.*

1 cup all-purpose flour
1 tablespoon granulated sugar
2 teaspoons baking powder
¼ teaspoon salt
1 cup milk
2 egg yolks
2 egg whites
　Cooking oil
　　(about 3 tablespoons)
　Jam, jelly, honey, syrup,
　　or applesauce (optional)
　Sifted powdered sugar
　　(optional)

1. In a mixing bowl combine flour, sugar, baking powder, and salt. In another mixing bowl stir together milk and egg yolks until well combined. Add to flour mixture. Stir until smooth.

2. In a small bowl beat egg whites with an electric mixer on high speed until stiff peaks form (tips stand straight). Gently fold beaten egg whites into batter, leaving a few puffs of egg white. Do not overbeat.

3. Place an aebleskiver pan over medium heat; lightly brush each cup with oil. When the oil sizzles, use about 2 tablespoons of the batter to fill each cup ⅔ full. Cook for 1 to 2 minutes. As a thin shell forms, use a fork or wooden toothpick to gently invert the cooked portion and allow the uncooked portion to flow into the cup. Invert each aebleskiver and cook until all shells are set and all sides are sealed. Continue rotating and cooking until they are evenly golden brown and a wooden toothpick inserted in their centers comes out clean.

4. Use a fork or wooden toothpick to transfer each aebleskiver to a plate. Serve immediately or keep warm in a loosely covered ovenproof dish in a 300° oven. If desired, serve with jam, jelly, honey, syrup, or applesauce and sprinkle with powdered sugar. Makes 30 aebleskiver.

Seasoning Cast Iron

*I*n order to prevent cast-iron cookware from rusting, it needs to be "seasoned" before its first use. Lightly rub the inside of a clean, dry pan with shortening. Wipe off the excess and heat the pan in a 250° to 300° oven for about an hour. To retain this seasoning between uses, wash seasoned cookware after each use in hot, sudsy water, but don't scour. Dry thoroughly immediately after washing. If rust develops, re-season the cookware.

Nutrition Facts per aebleskiver: 37 calories, 2 g total fat (0 g saturated fat), 15 mg cholesterol, 50 mg sodium, 4 g carbohydrates, 0 g fiber, 1 g protein
Daily Values: 2% vit. A, 0% vit. C, 2% calcium, 1% iron

Danish Aebleskiver

Kaiserschmarrn

(Emperor's Pancake)

Serve this sweet pancake, inspired by Austrian-Hungarian Emperor Franz Josef I, dusted with lots of powdered sugar.

Prep: 20 minutes
Bake: 15 minutes
Oven: 400°
Cool: 10 minutes
Makes 8 servings

¼ cup raisins
2 tablespoons rum
2 egg yolks
2 tablespoons granulated sugar
½ teaspoon vanilla
   Dash salt
1 cup all-purpose flour
⅔ cup milk
2 tablespoons margarine or
   butter, melted
2 egg whites
2 tablespoons granulated sugar
   Sifted powdered sugar
   Applesauce or jam
   (optional)

1. In a small bowl combine raisins and rum. Set aside to soak; do not drain.

2. In a large mixing bowl beat egg yolks, 2 tablespoons granulated sugar, vanilla, and salt with an electric mixer until thick and lemon-colored. Add flour and milk alternately to yolk mixture, beating on low speed after each addition until batter is smooth. Stir in the undrained raisin mixture and melted margarine or butter.

3. Wash beaters thoroughly. In a small mixing bowl beat egg whites with an electric mixer on medium to high speed until soft peaks form (tips curl). Gradually add 2 tablespoons granulated sugar, beating on high speed until stiff peaks form (tips stand straight). Gently fold beaten egg whites into egg yolk mixture, leaving a few puffs of egg white. Do not overbeat.

4. Generously grease a 10-inch ovenproof skillet. Pour batter into the skillet. Immediately place skillet in a 400° oven. Bake about 15 minutes or until pancake is golden brown. Let cool in pan 10 minutes. Invert pancake onto serving platter. Sprinkle generously with powdered sugar. Cut into pieces. If desired, serve with applesauce or jam. Makes 8 servings.

Nutrition Facts per serving: 157 calories, 5 g total fat (1 g saturated fat), 55 mg cholesterol, 77 mg sodium, 23 g carbohydrates, 1 g fiber, 4 g protein
Daily Values: 12% vit. A, 0% vit. C, 3% calcium, 6% iron

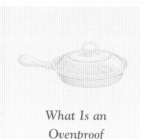

What Is an Ovenproof Skillet?

If your skillet has a wooden or plastic handle, it is not ovenproof. You can improvise by wrapping your skillet's handle in several layers of aluminum foil. This will protect it from the intense oven heat.

Fruit Blintzes

The blintz, similar to the French crepe, is of Russian-Polish origin. Instead of sweet fillings, blintzes often are filled with leftover shredded meat.

Prep: 50 minutes
Bake: 20 minutes
Oven: 400°
Makes 8 servings

Blintzes

¾ cup all-purpose flour
2 tablespoons granulated sugar
1 teaspoon baking powder
½ teaspoon salt
⅔ cup milk
⅓ cup water
2 eggs, slightly beaten
½ teaspoon vanilla

Filling

1 12-ounce can strawberry or other fruit cake-and-pastry filling
½ cup chopped pecans or almonds, toasted
3 to 4 teaspoons amaretto or ¼ teaspoon almond extract

Nonstick spray coating
2 tablespoons margarine or butter, melted
Sifted powdered sugar (optional)
Dairy sour cream or sweetened whipped cream (optional)

1. In a mixing bowl combine flour, granulated sugar, baking powder, and salt. In another mixing bowl, beat milk, water, eggs, and vanilla until well combined. Add to flour mixture; beat until smooth.

2. Heat a lightly greased 6-inch skillet over medium heat until a few drops of water dance across the surface. Remove skillet from heat. For each blintz, spoon a scant 2 tablespoons batter into hot skillet. Quickly lift and tilt skillet to spread batter into a thin, even circle. Cook about 1 minute or until top is set and edges are lightly browned. Invert skillet to remove blintz. Repeat with remaining batter, greasing skillet occasionally, to make 16 blintzes.

3. For filling, combine strawberry cake-and-pastry filling, nuts, and amaretto; stir until well combined.

4. To assemble, spray a 13×9×2-inch baking pan with nonstick coating. Place blintzes on a work surface, browned sides down; spoon about 1½ tablespoons of the filling in the middle of each blintz. Fold the top edge of each blintz over filling. Fold sides over, then fold bottom edges up over all. Place blintzes, seam sides down, in prepared baking pan. Brush with melted margarine. Bake in a 400° oven for 20 to 25 minutes or until heated through. If desired, top with powdered sugar and serve with sour cream or whipped cream. Makes 8 servings.

Nutrition Facts per serving: 257 calories, 9 g total fat (2 g saturated fat), 55 mg cholesterol, 263 mg sodium, 36 g carbohydrates, 3 g fiber, 4 g protein
Daily Values: 7% vit. A, 0% vit. C, 6% calcium, 13% iron

Blueberry-Ricotta Pancakes

Prep: 20 minutes
Makes 16 pancakes

For a creamy, delicious topping, try sweetened ricotta cheese. Combine 1 cup ricotta cheese and 2 tablespoons powdered sugar; cook over low heat just until warm.

½ **cup all-purpose flour**
2 **teaspoons baking powder**
½ **teaspoon salt**
1 **cup ricotta cheese**
4 **egg yolks**
3 **tablespoons sugar**
¼ **cup milk**
1½ **cups fresh or frozen blueberries**
4 **egg whites**
1 **recipe Blueberry Syrup (see page 94) (optional)**

1. In a mixing bowl combine flour, baking powder, and salt. In another mixing bowl beat together ricotta cheese, egg yolks, and sugar until well combined. Add to flour mixture; stir until smooth. Stir in milk. Fold in blueberries.

2. In a small mixing bowl beat the egg whites with an electric mixer on high speed until stiff peaks form (tips stand straight). Gently fold the beaten egg whites into batter, leaving a few puffs of egg white. Do not overbeat.

3. Heat a lightly greased griddle or heavy skillet over medium heat until a few drops of water dance across the surface. For each pancake, pour about ¼ cup batter onto the hot griddle. Spread batter into a circle about 4 inches in diameter.

4. Cook over medium heat until pancakes are golden brown, turning to cook the second sides when pancake surfaces are bubbly and edges are slightly dry (about 1 to 2 minutes per side). Serve immediately or keep warm in a loosely covered ovenproof dish in a 300° oven. If desired, serve with Blueberry Syrup. Makes 16 pancakes.

Nutrition Facts per pancake: 72 calories, 3 g total fat (1 g saturated fat), 58 mg cholesterol, 150 mg sodium, 8 g carbohydrates, 0 g fiber, 4 g protein
Daily Values: 10% vit. A, 3% vit. C, 8% calcium, 3% iron

Blueberry-Ricotta Pancakes with Blueberry Syrup

Peach Pancakes

Prep: 15 minutes
Makes 12 pancakes

Delight luncheon guests with these pancakes accompanied by slices of a mild-flavored cheese, such as Swiss or cheddar.

1 ½ **cups all-purpose flour**
  3 **tablespoons sugar**
  2 **teaspoons baking powder**
 ½ **teaspoon salt**
  2 **eggs, slightly beaten**
  1 **cup milk**
  3 **tablespoons margarine**
    or butter, melted
  1 **16-ounce can peach slices,**
    drained and very finely
    chopped, or 2 cups very
    finely chopped, peeled
    peaches

1. In a mixing bowl combine flour, sugar, baking powder, and salt. In another mixing bowl combine eggs, milk, and margarine or butter. Add to the flour mixture. Stir just until combined but still slightly lumpy. Fold in peaches.

2. Heat a lightly greased griddle or heavy skillet over medium heat until a few drops of water dance across the surface. For each pancake, pour about ¼ cup batter onto the hot griddle. Spread batter into a circle about 4 inches in diameter.

3. Cook over medium heat until pancakes are golden brown, turning to cook second sides when pancake surfaces are bubbly and edges are slightly dry (about 1 to 2 minutes per side). Serve immediately or keep warm in a loosely covered ovenproof dish in a 300° oven. Makes 12 pancakes.

Nutrition Facts per pancake: 131 calories, 4 g total fat (1 g saturated fat), 37 mg cholesterol, 206 mg sodium, 20 g carbohydrates, 1 g fiber, 3 g protein
Daily Values: 7% vit. A, 2% vit. C, 7% calcium, 6% iron

Dried Fruit Pancakes: Prepare as above, except substitute ½ cup finely snipped *dried apricots or dried apples* for the peaches. Top with *dairy sour cream or plain yogurt.*

Apple Griddle Cakes

*Serve these pancakes with your favorite sausage links and a splash of
Orange-Molasses Syrup (see recipe, page 97).*

Prep: 15 minutes
Makes 16 pancakes

1½ **cups finely chopped,
      peeled apples**
  2 **teaspoons lemon juice**
1½ **cups all-purpose flour**
  2 **tablespoons sugar**
  2 **teaspoons baking powder**
  ½ **teaspoon ground cinnamon**
  ¼ **teaspoon salt**
  1 **egg, slightly beaten**
1½ **cups milk**
  3 **tablespoons cooking oil or
      margarine or butter,
      melted**

1. In a small bowl combine apples and lemon juice; set aside. In a mixing bowl combine flour, sugar, baking powder, cinnamon, and salt. In another mixing bowl combine egg, milk, and oil or melted margarine or butter. Add to flour mixture. Stir just until combined but still slightly lumpy. Fold in apple mixture.

2. Heat a lightly greased griddle or heavy skillet over medium heat until a few drops of water dance across the surface. For each pancake, pour a scant ¼ cup batter onto the hot griddle. Spread batter into a circle about 4 inches in diameter.

3. Cook over medium heat until pancakes are golden brown, turning to cook second sides when pancake surfaces are bubbly and edges are slightly dry (about 1 to 2 minutes per side). Serve immediately or keep warm in a loosely covered ovenproof dish in a 300° oven. Makes 16 pancakes.

Nutrition Facts per pancake: 91 calories, 3 g total fat (1 g saturated fat), 15 mg cholesterol, 94 mg sodium, 13 g carbohydrates, 0 g fiber, 2 g protein
Daily Values: 2% vit. A, 1% vit. C, 6% calcium, 4% iron

Pancake Lore

A recipe for jelly pancakes in an old cookbook calls for pancakes to be baked, topped with jelly, rolled, and dredged in sugar. Then the cook is to use a red-hot toaster to burn lines on the sugared pancakes for an attractive appearance and the taste-tempting hint of caramelized sugar.

Tropical Fruit Pancakes

Tropical Fruit Pancakes

Prep: 20 minutes
Makes 20 pancakes

2 ripe bananas, sliced
2 teaspoons lemon juice
1¼ cups all-purpose flour
2 tablespoons sugar
2 teaspoons baking powder
½ teaspoon salt
1 cup milk
2 egg yolks
3 tablespoons margarine or
    butter, melted
1 8-ounce can crushed
    pineapple (juice pack),
    drained
2 egg whites
1 cup flaked coconut, toasted
  Cream cheese (optional)
  Sliced papaya, mango,
    banana, and/or pineapple
    (optional)

1. In a food processor bowl or blender container combine sliced bananas and lemon juice. Cover and process or blend until smooth. In a mixing bowl combine flour, sugar, baking powder, and salt. In another mixing bowl combine milk, egg yolks, and margarine or butter; stir in banana mixture and pineapple. Add banana mixture to flour mixture all at once. Stir just until batter is combined but still slightly lumpy.

2. In a small mixing bowl beat egg whites with an electric mixer on medium to high speed until stiff peaks form (tips stand straight). Gently fold egg whites and ⅔ *cup* of the coconut into the batter, leaving a few puffs of egg white. Do not overbeat.

3. Heat a lightly greased griddle or heavy skillet over medium heat until a few drops of water dance across the surface. For each pancake, pour about ¼ cup batter onto the hot griddle. Spread batter into a circle about 4 inches in diameter.

4. Cook over medium heat until pancakes are golden brown, turning to cook second sides when pancake surfaces are bubbly and edges are slightly dry (about 1 to 2 minutes per side). Serve immediately sprinkled with remaining coconut. If desired, top pancakes with cream cheese and fruit. Makes 20 pancakes.

Nutrition Facts per pancake: 99 calories, 4 g total fat (1 g saturated fat), 22 mg cholesterol, 131 mg sodium, 14 g carbohydrates, 0 g fiber, 2 g protein
Daily Values: 6% vit. A, 4% vit. C, 4% calcium, 4% iron

Cranberry Pancakes

To decrease preparation time, whirl your cranberries in a food processor or blender.

Prep: 15 minutes
Makes 16 pancakes

Pancake Lore

*ate in the
19th century
one cookbook
suggested: The nicest
way to grease a
griddle is to rub a
large piece of beef
suet tied in a thin
cloth over the hot
griddle. A piece of
pork an inch square
run on a tin fork is
another suitable
griddle greaser.*

1½ **cups cranberries, coarsely chopped**
¼ **cup sugar**
2 **teaspoons finely shredded orange peel**
1½ **cups all-purpose flour**
2 **teaspoons baking powder**
½ **teaspoon baking soda**
½ **teaspoon salt**
1 **egg, slightly beaten**
1 **cup buttermilk**
½ **cup orange juice**
3 **tablespoons margarine or butter, melted**
1 **recipe Cranberry Syrup (see page 96) (optional)**

1. In a small mixing bowl combine cranberries, sugar, and orange peel; set aside. In a large mixing bowl combine flour, baking powder, baking soda, and salt. In another mixing bowl combine egg, buttermilk, orange juice, and margarine or butter. Add to flour mixture. Stir just until combined but still slightly lumpy. Fold in cranberry mixture.

2. Heat a lightly greased griddle or heavy skillet over medium heat until a few drops of water dance across the surface. For each pancake, pour about ¼ cup batter onto the hot griddle.

3. Cook over medium heat until pancakes are golden brown, turning to cook second sides when pancake surfaces are bubbly and edges are slightly dry (about 1 to 2 minutes per side). Serve immediately or keep warm in a loosely covered ovenproof dish in a 300° oven. If desired, serve with Cranberry Syrup. Makes 16 pancakes.

Nutrition Facts per pancake: 90 calories, 3 g total fat (1 g saturated fat), 14 mg cholesterol, 197 mg sodium, 14 g carbohydrates, 1 g fiber, 2 g protein
Daily Values: 3% vit. A, 9% vit. C, 5% calcium, 4% iron

Nutty Cranberry Pancakes: Prepare as above, except stir ½ cup chopped *walnuts* into batter.

Banana Pancakes

Mashed bananas make these pancakes rich-tasting, moist, and tender. They're scrumptious served with flavored yogurt or an assortment of fresh fruit.

Prep: 15 minutes
Makes 16 pancakes

1¾ cups all-purpose flour
1 tablespoon sugar
1½ teaspoons baking powder
½ teaspoon salt
¼ teaspoon ground cinnamon
2 eggs, slightly beaten
2 cups milk
2 ripe medium bananas,
    mashed (about ¾ cup)
3 tablespoons margarine
    or butter, melted, or
    cooking oil
⅓ cup finely chopped walnuts
    or pecans

1. In a mixing bowl combine flour, sugar, baking powder, salt, and cinnamon. In another mixing bowl combine eggs, milk, bananas, and melted margarine or butter or oil. Add to the flour mixture. Stir just until combined but still slightly lumpy. Stir in walnuts or pecans.

2. Heat a lightly greased griddle or heavy skillet over medium heat until a few drops of water dance across the surface. For each pancake, pour about ¼ cup batter onto the hot griddle.

3. Cook over medium heat until pancakes are golden brown, turning to cook second sides when pancake surfaces are bubbly and edges are slightly dry (about 1 to 2 minutes per side). Serve immediately or keep warm in a loosely covered ovenproof dish in a 300° oven. Makes 16 pancakes.

Nutrition Facts per pancake: 122 calories, 5 g total fat (1 g saturated fat), 29 mg cholesterol, 150 mg sodium, 16 g carbohydrates, 1 g fiber, 4 g protein
Daily Values: 5% vit. A, 2% vit. C, 6% calcium, 5% iron

Go Bananas

Overripe bananas are perfect for cooking and baking. Mash the bananas, place about 1 cup in a small, sealable freezer bag, and freeze. A package thaws easily in the refrigerator overnight. Besides flavoring pancake batters, thawed banana works great in blended fruit drinks and breads.

Buckwheat and Pear Pancakes

Prep: 15 minutes
Makes 24 pancakes

An 8-ounce can of pears, drained and chopped, can be substituted for the fresh pear in these flavorful pancakes.

2 cups **Buckwheat Pancake Mix (see page 89)**
1¾ **cups milk**
2 **eggs, slightly beaten**
2 **tablespoons cooking oil**
1 **teaspoon vanilla**
1 **cup chopped, peeled pear**

1. In a mixing bowl combine Buckwheat Pancake Mix, milk, eggs, oil, and vanilla. Stir just until combined but still slightly lumpy. Stir in pear.

2. Heat a lightly greased griddle or heavy skillet over medium heat until a few drops of water dance across the surface. For each pancake, pour a scant ¼ cup batter onto the hot griddle. Spread batter into a circle about 4 inches in diameter.

3. Cook over medium heat until pancakes are golden brown, turning to cook second sides when pancake surfaces are bubbly and edges are slightly dry (about 1 to 2 minutes per side). Serve immediately or keep warm in a loosely covered ovenproof dish in a 300° oven. Makes 24 pancakes.

Nutrition Facts per pancake: 67 calories, 2 g total fat (1 g saturated fat), 19 mg cholesterol, 152 mg sodium, 10 g carbohydrates, 2 g fiber, 2 g protein
Daily Values: 1% vit. A, 0% vit. C, 4% calcium, 3% iron

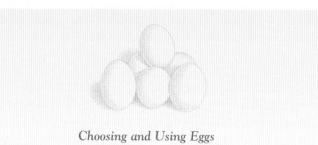

Choosing and Using Eggs

Eggs, like any perishable food, require careful storage and handling. Follow these guidelines to ensure safe eating.

- *Purchase clean, fresh eggs from refrigerated display cases.*
- *At home, refrigerate eggs promptly in their original carton.*
- *Do not wash eggs before storing or using.*
- *Discard eggs with cracked shells.*
- *For best quality, use refrigerated, raw, whole eggs within 1 week. You can store them safely, however, for as long as 5 weeks. Use leftover yolks and whites within 4 days.*

Pineapple Pancakes

Prep: 15 minutes
Makes 20 pancakes

2 cups all-purpose flour
2 tablespoons brown sugar
1 tablespoon baking powder
¼ teaspoon baking soda
¼ teaspoon salt
2 eggs, slightly beaten
1 20-ounce can crushed
    pineapple (juice pack)
¾ cup milk
¼ cup margarine or butter,
    melted
1 recipe Pineapple Sauce
    (see page 107) (optional)

1. In a mixing bowl combine flour, brown sugar, baking powder, baking soda, and salt. In another mixing bowl combine eggs, undrained pineapple, milk, and margarine or butter. Add to flour mixture. Stir just until combined but still slightly lumpy.

2. Heat a lightly greased griddle or heavy skillet over medium heat until a few drops of water dance across the surface. For each pancake, pour about ¼ cup batter onto the hot griddle. Spread batter into a circle about 4 inches in diameter.

3. Cook over medium heat until pancakes are golden brown, turning to cook second sides when pancake surfaces are bubbly and edges are slightly dry (about 1½ to 2 minutes per side). Serve immediately or keep warm in a loosely covered ovenproof dish in a 300° oven. If desired, serve with Pineapple Sauce. Makes 20 pancakes.

Nutrition Facts per pancake: 94 calories, 3 g total fat (1 g saturated fat), 22 mg cholesterol, 135 mg sodium, 14 g carbohydrates, 0 g fiber, 2 g protein
Daily Values: 4% vit. A, 4% vit. C, 5% calcium, 5% iron

Fresh Corn Pancakes

For variety, try stirring some crumbled, cooked bacon into the batter.

Prep: 15 minutes
Makes 12 pancakes

1 egg, slightly beaten
1 cup milk
2 tablespoons margarine or
    butter, melted
1/8 teaspoon pepper
1 1/2 cups Buttermilk Pancake
    Mix (see page 80)
2 cups cut fresh corn
    (about 4 ears) or frozen
    whole kernel corn
1/4 cup thinly sliced
    green onion
1/4 cup finely chopped red or
    green sweet pepper
1 recipe Herb Butter
    (see page 102) (optional)

1. In a mixing bowl combine egg, milk, margarine or butter, and pepper. Add Buttermilk Pancake Mix. Stir just until combined but still slightly lumpy. Fold in corn, green onion, and sweet pepper.

2. Heat a lightly greased griddle or heavy skillet over medium heat until a few drops of water dance across the surface. For each pancake, pour about 1/4 cup batter onto the hot griddle. Spread batter into a circle about 4 inches in diameter. (For a smaller pancake as in the photo on page 37, spread about 2 tablespoons batter into a circle about 2 inches in diameter.)

3. Cook over medium heat until pancakes are golden brown, turning to cook second sides when pancake surfaces are bubbly and edges are slightly dry (about 2 to 3 minutes per side). Serve immediately or keep warm in a loosely covered ovenproof dish in a 300° oven. If desired, serve with Herb Butter. Makes twelve 4-inch pancakes or twenty-four 2-inch pancakes.

Nutrition Facts per 4-inch pancake: 252 calories, 5 g total fat (1 g saturated fat), 21 mg cholesterol, 217 mg sodium, 50 g carbohydrates, 6 g fiber, 8 g protein
Daily Values: 9% vit. A, 22% vit. C, 8% calcium, 10% iron

Beating Egg Whites to Stiff Peaks

Many of the recipes in this cookbook require beaten egg whites. Here's how to do it: Place egg whites in a clean glass or metal bowl. (Don't use plastic or wooden bowls as they can absorb fat, which isn't easily washed out, and this fat may keep egg whites from beating up properly.) Beat egg whites with an electric mixer on medium to high speed or a rotary beater until the egg whites form stiff peaks (tips that stand straight up when the beaters are lifted out of the bowl).

Fresh Corn Pancakes

Beet Pancakes

Prep: 15 minutes
Makes 16 pancakes

A perfect accompaniment to roast beef, these pink pancakes also are good when served with Horseradish-Parsley Butter (see page 103).

1½ **cups all-purpose flour**
1 **teaspoon baking powder**
½ **teaspoon baking soda**
½ **teaspoon salt**
2 **eggs, slightly beaten**
1½ **cups buttermilk**
2 **tablespoons margarine or butter, melted**
1 **14½-ounce can diced beets, drained (about 1½ cups)**
 Milk (optional)
1 **recipe Sour Cream-Horseradish Sauce (see below) (optional)**

1. In a mixing bowl combine flour, baking powder, baking soda, and salt. In another mixing bowl combine eggs, buttermilk, and margarine or butter. Add to flour mixture. Stir just until combined but still slightly lumpy. Stir in the beets. (If batter is too thick, add milk, 1 tablespoon at a time, until desired consistency is reached).

2. Heat a lightly greased griddle or heavy skillet over medium heat until a few drops of water dance across the surface. For each pancake, pour about ¼ cup batter onto the hot griddle. Spread batter into a circle about 4 inches in diameter. (For a smaller pancake, spread about 2 tablespoons batter into a circle about 2 inches in diameter.)

3. Cook over medium heat until pancakes are golden brown, turning to cook second sides when pancake surfaces are bubbly and edges are slightly dry (about 1 to 2 minutes per side). Serve immediately or keep warm in a loosely covered ovenproof dish in a 300° oven. If desired, serve with Sour Cream-Horseradish Sauce. Makes about sixteen 4-inch pancakes or thirty-two 2-inch pancakes.

Sour Cream-Horseradish Sauce: In a small bowl stir together ½ cup *dairy sour cream* and 1 to 2 teaspoons *prepared horseradish*.

Nutrition Facts per 4-inch pancake: 76 calories, 2 g total fat (1 g saturated fat), 27 mg cholesterol, 221 mg sodium, 11 g carbohydrates, 1 g fiber, 3 g protein
Daily Values: 3% vit. A, 1% vit. C, 4% calcium, 6% iron

Buttermilk Substitutes

*I*f you don't have any buttermilk on hand, sour milk is a good alternative. For each cup of soured milk desired, in a glass measuring cup combine 1 tablespoon lemon juice or vinegar and enough milk to total 1 cup of liquid. Stir well and let stand for 5 minutes before using.

You also can substitute powdered buttermilk for fresh. Simply follow the package directions.

Potato and Corn Pancakes

Potato soup and frozen corn speed the preparation of these tasty pancakes.

Prep: 15 minutes
Makes 10 pancakes

1 10¾-ounce can condensed
    cream of potato soup
⅓ cup all-purpose flour
3 eggs, slightly beaten
2 tablespoons margarine or
    butter, melted
½ cup frozen whole kernel
    corn, thawed
1 tablespoon finely
    chopped onion
2 slices bacon, crisp-cooked,
    drained, and crumbled,
    or 2 tablespoons cooked
    bacon pieces (optional)
Applesauce (optional)

1. In a medium mixing bowl combine soup and flour; stir in eggs and margarine or butter. Fold in corn, onion, and, if desired, bacon.

2. Heat a lightly greased griddle or heavy skillet over medium heat until a few drops of water dance across the surface. For each pancake, pour about ¼ cup batter onto the hot griddle. Spread batter into a circle about 4 inches in diameter.

3. Cook over medium heat until pancakes are golden brown, turning to cook second sides when pancake surfaces are bubbly and edges are slightly dry (about 1 to 2 minutes per side). Serve immediately or keep warm in a loosely covered ovenproof dish in a 300° oven. If desired, serve with applesauce. Makes 10 pancakes.

Nutrition Facts per pancake: 81 calories, 4 g total fat (1 g saturated fat), 65 mg cholesterol, 289 mg sodium, 8 g carbohydrates, 0 g fiber, 3 g protein
Daily Values: 6% vit. A, 0% vit. C, 1% calcium, 3% iron

Potato Pancakes

Try serving some whole ripe olives alongside these crisp-cooked pancakes.

Prep: 15 minutes
Stand: 15 minutes
Makes 9 pancakes

4 medium potatoes, peeled
   (about 1⅓ pounds)
1 medium onion
½ teaspoon salt
¼ cup chopped pitted ripe
   olives, chopped green
   sweet pepper, diced ham,
   or finely chopped canned
   mushrooms (optional)
2 eggs, slightly beaten
2 tablespoons all-purpose flour
⅛ teaspoon pepper
¼ cup cooking oil
¼ cup dairy sour cream
   (optional)

1. Line a baking sheet with paper towels; set aside. Finely shred potatoes into a bowl of cold water; drain. Finely shred onion; add to potatoes along with the salt. Place the potato mixture in a colander set over a large bowl. Let the mixture stand for 15 minutes, stirring occasionally. Press the potato mixture firmly to remove as much liquid as possible. Discard the liquid. Transfer the potato mixture to a large mixing bowl. If desired, stir in olives, sweet pepper, ham, or mushrooms.

2. In a small mixing bowl combine the eggs, flour, and pepper. Add to the potato mixture; mix well.

3. Heat oil in a heavy skillet over medium heat until hot (add additional oil as needed). For each pancake, drop about ¼ cup potato mixture into the hot skillet. Spread mixture into a circle about 4 inches in diameter.

4. Cook over medium heat for 2 to 3 minutes per side or until pancakes are crisp and golden brown (reduce heat if pancakes are browning too fast). Drain pancakes briefly on the prepared baking sheet. Serve immediately or keep warm in a loosely covered ovenproof dish in a 300° oven. If desired, serve with sour cream. Makes 9 pancakes.

Nutrition Facts per pancake: 111 calories, 5 g total fat (1 g saturated fat), 47 mg cholesterol, 136 mg sodium, 14 g carbohydrates, 1 g fiber, 3 g protein
Daily Values: 2% vit. A, 8% vit. C, 1% calcium, 2% iron

Sweet Potato Pancakes

*The rich orange color and mild flavor of sweet potatoes provide an
eye-catching alternative to traditional pancakes.*

Prep: 25 minutes
Makes 15 pancakes

1¼ cups all-purpose flour
2 tablespoons sugar
1¼ teaspoons baking powder
¾ teaspoon salt
2 eggs, slightly beaten
1¼ cups milk
½ cup mashed cooked sweet
 potatoes, cooled
3 tablespoons margarine or
 butter, melted
1 recipe Spiced Syrup
 (see page 95) (optional)

1. In a mixing bowl combine flour, sugar, baking
powder, and salt. In another mixing bowl combine
eggs, milk, sweet potatoes, and margarine or butter.
Add to flour mixture. Stir just until combined but
still slightly lumpy.

2. Heat a lightly greased griddle or heavy skillet
over medium heat until a few drops of water dance
across the surface. For each pancake, pour about
¼ cup batter onto the hot griddle.

3. Cook over medium heat until pancakes are
golden brown, turning to cook second sides when
pancake surfaces are bubbly and edges are slightly dry
(about 1 to 2 minutes per side). Serve immediately or
keep warm in a loosely covered ovenproof dish in a
300° oven. If desired, serve with Spiced Syrup.
Makes 15 pancakes.

Nutrition Facts per pancake: 86 calories, 3 g total fat (1 g saturated fat),
30 mg cholesterol, 183 mg sodium, 11 g carbohydrates, 0 g fiber, 3 g protein
Daily Values: 14% vit. A, 1% vit. C, 5% calcium, 4% iron

Sweet Potatoes Or Yams?

*Yams are a
tropically
grown tuber with
brownish skin and
yellow to white
starchy flesh. They
are not widely
available in the
United States and
many times the
vegetables in
supermarkets labeled
yams are actually a
type of sweet potato.
Either will work in
this recipe.*

Zucchini Pancake

Zucchini Pancake

*Versatile zucchini works mealtime magic in a variety of dishes, including pancakes.
Serve these colorful pancakes for a light Sunday night supper with a
tossed salad and your favorite dessert.*

Prep: 30 minutes
Bake: 20 minutes
Oven: 400°
Makes 6 servings

¾ cup shredded zucchini
   Nonstick spray coating
⅓ cup all-purpose flour
½ teaspoon baking powder
¼ teaspoon garlic salt
4 egg yolks
⅓ cup milk
½ cup finely shredded
   Parmesan cheese
½ cup shredded carrot
½ cup finely chopped red or
   green sweet pepper
¼ cup finely chopped onion
4 egg whites
   Finely shredded Parmesan
   cheese (optional)

1. Pat zucchini dry between paper towels; set aside. Spray a 2-quart rectangular baking dish with nonstick coating; set dish aside.

2. In a large mixing bowl combine flour, baking powder, and garlic salt. Beat in egg yolks and milk until smooth. Stir in zucchini, Parmesan cheese, carrot, sweet pepper, and onion.

3. In a medium mixing bowl beat egg whites with an electric mixer on medium to high speed until stiff peaks form (tips stand straight). Gently fold beaten egg whites into batter, leaving in a few puffs of egg white. Do not overbeat. Pour batter into prepared baking dish, spreading to edges.

4. Bake in a 400° oven about 20 minutes or until a knife inserted near the center comes out clean. To serve, cut into squares. If desired, sprinkle with additional Parmesan cheese. Makes 6 servings.

Make-Ahead Directions: Prepare as above. Cover and chill for up to 2 hours before baking. Continue as directed.

Nutrition Facts per serving: 129 calories, 6 g total fat (1g saturated fat),
150 mg cholesterol, 274 mg sodium, 9 g carbohydrates, 1 g fiber, 9 g protein
Daily Values: 55% vit. A, 26% vit. C, 12% calcium, 5% iron

Crunchy Vegetable and Rice Pancakes

Prep: 25 minutes
Makes 12 pancakes

*Delicious, inexpensive, and full of good, crisp vegetables, enjoy these
Oriental-flavored pancakes any time.*

1 cup finely shredded cabbage
1 cup cooked brown rice
½ cup bean sprouts, chopped
¼ cup all-purpose flour
¼ cup finely chopped onion
¼ cup finely chopped red or
 green sweet pepper
½ teaspoon celery seed
4 eggs, slightly beaten
1 tablespoon reduced-sodium
 soy sauce
¼ teaspoon pepper
1 recipe Chinese Sauce
 (see below)

1. In a mixing bowl combine cabbage, cooked brown rice, bean sprouts, flour, onion, sweet pepper, and celery seed. In another mixing bowl combine eggs, soy sauce, and pepper. Add to cabbage mixture. Stir just until combined but still slightly lumpy.

2. Heat a lightly greased griddle or heavy skillet over medium heat until a few drops of water dance across the surface. For each pancake, pour about ¼ cup batter onto the hot griddle. Spread batter into a circle about 4 inches in diameter.

3. Cook over medium heat until pancakes are golden brown, turning to cook second sides when pancake surfaces are bubbly and edges are slightly dry (about 2 to 3 minutes per side). Serve immediately or keep warm in a loosely covered ovenproof dish in a 300° oven. Serve with Chinese Sauce. Makes 12 pancakes.

Chinese Sauce: In a small saucepan stir together 1 cup *reduced-sodium chicken broth* and 1 tablespoon *cornstarch*. Cook and stir over medium heat until thickened and bubbly. Cook and stir for 2 minutes more. Stir in 1½ teaspoons *reduced-sodium soy sauce* and ½ teaspoon grated *gingerroot* or ⅛ teaspoon *ground ginger*; heat through. Serve warm. Makes about ¾ cup.

Nutrition Facts per pancake with 1 tablespoon sauce: 63 calories, 2 g total fat (1g saturated fat), 71 mg cholesterol, 143 mg sodium, 8 g carbohydrates, 1 g fiber, 3 g protein
Daily Values: 4% vit. A, 12% vit. C, 1% calcium, 4% iron

Spinach and Cheese Pancakes

Team these robust pancakes with grilled chicken or fish.

Prep: 20 minutes
Makes 10 pancakes

¼ cup finely chopped onion
1 clove garlic, minced
1 tablespoon margarine
  or butter
½ cup milk
4 eggs, slightly beaten
⅛ teaspoon pepper
¼ teaspoon dried thyme,
  crushed
1 10-ounce package frozen
  spinach, thawed and
  well drained
1 cup fine dry bread crumbs
¼ cup finely shredded
  Parmesan cheese
1 tablespoon olive oil
  Plain low-fat yogurt, dairy
  sour cream, or finely
  shredded Parmesan cheese
  (optional)

1. In a small skillet cook onion and garlic in margarine or butter over medium heat until tender but not brown; set aside. In a large mixing bowl combine the milk, eggs, pepper, and thyme. Stir in spinach, bread crumbs, and the ¼ cup Parmesan cheese; add onion mixture and olive oil.

2. Heat a lightly greased griddle or heavy skillet over medium heat until a few drops of water dance across the surface. For each pancake, drop about ¼ cup batter onto the hot griddle (batter will be thick). Spread batter into a circle about 4 inches in diameter.

3. Cook over medium heat until pancakes are golden brown, turning to cook second sides when pancake surfaces are bubbly and edges are slightly dry (about 2 to 3 minutes per side). Serve immediately or keep warm in a loosely covered ovenproof dish in a 300° oven. If desired, top with yogurt, sour cream, or Parmesan cheese. Makes 10 pancakes.

Nutrition Facts per pancake: 115 calories, 6 g total fat (1 g saturated fat), 88 mg cholesterol, 167 mg sodium, 10 g carbohydrates, 0 g fiber, 6 g protein
Daily Values: 21% vit. A, 4% vit. C, 7% calcium, 6% iron

Pancake Lore

If you throw pancakes to the rooster and he eats them without calling the hens, you will remain single. If he calls the hens, you will marry.

Tomato Pancakes

Tomato Pancakes

1¾ cups water
2 eggs, slightly beaten
4 cups Oatmeal Pancake Mix
(see page 86)
2 cups finely chopped
seeded tomatoes
1 cup finely chopped green
sweet pepper
¾ to 1½ cups shredded
cheddar, Monterey Jack,
or American cheese
(optional)

1. In a large mixing bowl combine water and eggs; add Oatmeal Pancake Mix. Stir just until combined but still slightly lumpy. Stir in tomatoes and sweet pepper. Let stand for 5 minutes.

2. Heat a lightly greased griddle or heavy skillet over medium heat until a few drops of water dance across the surface. For each pancake, pour about ¼ cup batter onto the hot griddle.

3. Cook over medium heat until pancakes are golden brown, turning to cook second sides when pancake surfaces are bubbly and edges are slightly dry (about 1 to 2 minutes per side). If desired, transfer pancakes to an ovenproof platter; sprinkle with cheese. Place in a 300° oven for 2 to 3 minutes or until cheese begins to melt. Makes 12 pancakes.

Nutrition Facts per pancake: 189 calories, 10 g total fat (3 g saturated fat), 36 mg cholesterol, 241 mg sodium, 20 g carbohydrates, 2 g fiber, 5 g protein
Daily Values: 6% vit. A, 22% vit. C, 13% calcium, 9% iron

Prep: 10 minutes
Stand: 5 minutes
Bake: 2 minutes
Oven: 300°
Makes 12 pancakes

Ricotta-and-Spinach-Filled Crepes

You can prepare these attractive, main-dish crepes the day before you want to serve them. Cover and refrigerate the filled crepes. When you're ready to bake them, add the sauce and cheeses and pop them in the oven for 25 to 30 minutes.

Prep: 1 hour
Bake: 20 minutes
Oven: 400°
Stand: 10 minutes
Makes 10 servings

20 **Basic Crepes (see page 61)**
   Nonstick spray coating
 1 **10-ounce package frozen**
   chopped spinach, thawed
   and well drained
 1 **teaspoon dried Italian**
   seasoning, crushed
⅛ **teaspoon pepper**
 1 **15-ounce container ricotta**
   cheese
½ **cup finely shredded**
   Parmesan cheese
 3 **eggs, slightly beaten**
 2 **cups purchased refrigerated**
   marinara or spaghetti
   sauce
¾ **cup shredded mozzarella**
   cheese

1. Prepare Basic Crepes; keep warm. Spray a 3-quart rectangular baking dish with nonstick coating; set dish aside.

2. For filling, squeeze as much water as possible from spinach. In a medium mixing bowl combine spinach, Italian seasoning, and pepper. Add ricotta cheese, ⅓ *cup* of the Parmesan cheese, and the eggs. Stir until well combined.

3. Spoon about 2 tablespoons of the filling down the center of each crepe; roll up jelly-roll style. Place crepes, seam sides down, in prepared baking dish. Pour marinara or spaghetti sauce over crepes. Top with mozzarella cheese. Sprinkle remaining Parmesan cheese evenly over the top.

4. Bake, uncovered, in a 400° oven about 20 minutes or until cheeses melt and crepes are heated through. Let stand 10 minutes before serving. Makes 10 servings.

Nutrition Facts per serving: 123 calories, 6 g total fat (2 g saturated fat), 76 mg cholesterol, 248 mg sodium, 9 g carbohydrates, 1 g fiber, 8 g protein
Daily Values: 16% vit. A, 5% vit. C, 13% calcium, 5% iron

Ricotta-and-Spinach-Filled Crepes

Ham and Cheese Pancake Sandwiches

Prep: 15 minutes
Bake: 7 minutes
Oven: 350°
Makes 8 sandwiches

John Montagu, the fourth Earl of Sandwich, achieved immortality because he was too busy at the gaming tables to stop for a proper meal. He developed the habit of sending for cold meat between two slices of bread so he could eat yet not interrupt his gambling. Others followed his lead, and the popularity of the "Sandwich" grew. Pancake sandwiches, a modern innovation, make a filling main dish served with either fruit preserves or mustard.

1 cup whole wheat flour
¾ cup all-purpose flour
2 tablespoons sugar
2 teaspoons baking powder
1 teaspoon baking soda
1 teaspoon salt
2 eggs, slightly beaten
2¼ cups buttermilk
3 tablespoons margarine or butter, melted
½ cup desired fruit preserves or creamy Dijon-style mustard blend
8 1-ounce slices fully cooked ham
8 1-ounce slices Swiss cheese

1. In a mixing bowl combine whole wheat flour, all-purpose flour, sugar, baking powder, baking soda, and salt. In another mixing bowl combine eggs, buttermilk, and melted margarine or butter. Add to flour mixture. Stir just until combined but still slightly lumpy.

2. Heat a lightly greased griddle or heavy skillet over medium heat until a few drops of water dance across the surface. For each pancake, pour about ¼ cup batter onto the hot griddle. Spread batter into a circle about 5 inches in diameter.

3. Cook over medium heat until pancakes are golden brown, turning to cook second sides when pancake surfaces are bubbly and edges are slightly dry (1 to 2 minutes per side).

4. To assemble, place 8 pancakes on a baking sheet; spread each with preserves or mustard blend. Place a slice of ham and a slice of cheese on each pancake. Top with another pancake. Bake in 350° oven for 7 to 8 minutes or until cheese melts and sandwiches are hot. Makes 8 pancake sandwiches.

Nutrition Facts per sandwich: 195 calories, 8 g total fat (4 g saturated fat), 48 mg cholesterol, 536 mg sodium, 21 g carbohydrates, 1 g fiber, 11 g protein
Daily Values: 7% vit. A, 5% vit. C, 19% calcium, 6% iron

Oven Pancake

This versatile recipe works as an easy-on-the-cook brunch pancake for eight or as a crust for a pizza at dinnertime.

Prep: 10 minutes
Bake: 10 minutes
Oven: 450°
Makes 8 servings

Nonstick spray coating
2 cups Buttermilk Pancake Mix (see page 80)
1 cup water
1 egg, slightly beaten
1 tablespoon cooking oil
¾ cup diced fully cooked ham

1. Lightly spray a 15½×10½×2-inch baking pan with nonstick coating; set aside.

2. In a large mixing bowl combine Buttermilk Pancake Mix, water, egg, and oil. Stir until smooth. Stir in ham. Pour batter into prepared baking pan; spread evenly out to the edges.

3. Bake in a 450° oven for 10 to 12 minutes or until top is golden brown and a toothpick inserted near the center comes out clean. To serve, cut into 8 pieces. Makes 8 servings.

Nutrition Facts per serving: 150 calories, 4 g total fat (1 g saturated fat), 37 mg cholesterol, 473 mg sodium, 21 g carbohydrates, 1 g fiber, 8 g protein
Daily Values: 1% vit. A, 5% vit. C, 11% calcium, 9% iron

Pizza on a Pancake: Prepare as above, except omit the ham. If desired, add 1 teaspoon *dried Italian seasoning*, crushed, to the batter. Bake as directed. Remove from oven; reduce oven temperature to 350°. Top baked pancake with one 15-ounce can *pizza sauce*, 1½ cups cooked *ground meat*, and 1½ cups shredded *mozzarella cheese*. Bake in the 350° oven about 10 minutes or until cheese melts and topping is heated through. Makes 8 servings.

Nonstick S-S-S-Spray Secret

Nonstick spray coating bypasses the mess of greasing pans. Even better, it contains only 0.8 grams of fat in a 1¼-second spray.

Here are a couple of secrets for success:
- *Think of a 1¼-second spray as replacing 1 tablespoon of margarine, butter, cooking oil, or shortening.*
- *Spray only onto cold skillets and baking pans because nonstick spray coating can burn or smoke if sprayed onto hot surfaces.*

Puff Pancake with Ham and Broccoli

Puff Pancake with Ham and Broccoli

Fill this popover-like pancake with a ham and broccoli combo or your own blend of vegetables and meat.

Prep: 10 minutes
Bake: 18 minutes
Oven: 450°
Makes 4 servings

Pancake

3 eggs
½ cup all-purpose flour
½ cup milk
2 tablespoons margarine or
    butter, melted
¼ teaspoon salt

Filling

¾ cup milk
2 tablespoons all-purpose flour
2 cups cooked broccoli
    flowerets
1 cup diced fully cooked ham
¼ cup light dairy sour cream
1 teaspoon lemon juice
1 tablespoon snipped fresh
    dill, basil, or thyme or
    ¼ teaspoon dried dillweed,
    basil, or thyme, crushed
¼ teaspoon bottled hot
    pepper sauce

1. In a medium mixing bowl beat eggs with a wire whisk until frothy. Add the ½ cup flour, the ½ cup milk, *1 tablespoon* of the margarine or butter, and the salt; beat until smooth.

2. Heat an 8×1½-inch round baking pan or an 8-inch ovenproof skillet in a 450° oven for 2 minutes. Add the remaining 1 tablespoon margarine or butter; swirl to coat pan. Pour batter into hot pan. Bake pancake in the 450° oven for 18 to 20 minutes or until puffed and golden.

3. Meanwhile, for filling, in a medium saucepan combine the ¾ cup milk and the 2 tablespoons flour. Cook over medium-low heat, stirring constantly, until mixture is thickened and bubbly. Cook and stir 1 minute more. Stir in broccoli; ham; sour cream; lemon juice; dill, basil, or thyme; and hot pepper sauce. Continue cooking over medium heat until heated through, stirring occasionally. Do not boil.

4. To serve, remove pancake from oven. Spoon filling into center of pancake. Cut into wedges. Pancake will collapse as it cools. Makes 4 servings.

Nutrition Facts per serving: 303 calories, 14 g total fat (4 g saturated fat), 186 mg cholesterol, 746 mg sodium, 24 g carbohydrates, 3 g fiber, 20 g protein
Daily Values: 31% vit. A, 111% vit. C, 14% calcium, 17% iron

Shrimp and Spinach Pancakes

Garnish this tasty brunch entrée with a light dusting of freshly grated Parmesan cheese.

Prep: 20 minutes
Makes 16 pancakes

8 ounces finely chopped fresh cooked shrimp or frozen, peeled, cooked shrimp, thawed (1½ cups)
1 cup chopped fresh spinach or ½ of a 10-ounce package frozen chopped spinach, thawed and well drained
2 tablespoons finely chopped green onion
1¾ cups all-purpose flour
1 tablespoon baking powder
¼ teaspoon salt
⅛ teaspoon pepper
2 eggs, slightly beaten
1⅓ cups milk
⅓ cup cooking oil
1 recipe Quick Tomato Sauce (see below) (optional)

1. In a small mixing bowl combine shrimp, spinach, and green onion; set aside. In a large mixing bowl combine flour, baking powder, salt, and pepper. In another mixing bowl combine eggs, milk, and oil. Add to the flour mixture. Stir just until combined but still slightly lumpy. Stir in spinach mixture.

2. Heat a lightly greased griddle or heavy skillet over medium heat until a few drops of water dance across the surface. For each pancake, pour about ¼ cup batter onto the hot griddle. Spread batter into a circle about 4 inches in diameter. (For a smaller pancake as in the photo on page 55, spread about 2 tablespoons batter into a circle about 2 inches in diameter.)

3. Cook over medium heat until pancakes are golden brown, turning to cook second sides when pancake surfaces are bubbly and edges are slightly dry (2 to 3 minutes per side). Serve immediately or keep warm in a loosely covered ovenproof dish in a 300° oven. If desired, serve with Quick Tomato Sauce. Makes sixteen 4-inch pancakes or thirty 2-inch pancakes.

Quick Tomato Sauce: In a small saucepan combine one 10¾-ounce can *condensed tomato soup*, ½ cup *milk*, 2 tablespoons *margarine or butter*, and ½ to 1 teaspoon *curry powder*. Cook over medium heat until margarine melts. Serve warm. Makes 2 cups.

Nutrition Facts per 4-inch pancake: 121 calories, 6 g total fat (1 g saturated fat), 56 mg cholesterol, 154 mg sodium, 11 g carbohydrates, 0 g fiber, 6 g protein
Daily Values: 5% vit. A, 2% vit. C, 8% calcium, 8% iron

Shrimp and Spinach Pancakes

Mushroom-Filled Crepes

Prep: 45 minutes
Makes 4 servings

*Rich, meaty shiitake mushrooms lend full-bodied flavor to this side dish.
Serve these crepes with a mixed green salad for a light lunch.*

8 **Basic Crepes (see page 61)**
1 **tablespoon margarine
    or butter**
3 **cups sliced fresh shiitake
    mushrooms or button
    mushrooms**
½ **cup chopped green onion**
1 **tablespoon snipped fresh
    rosemary or thyme or**
    ½ **teaspoon dried rosemary
    or thyme, crushed**
¼ **teaspoon lemon-pepper
    seasoning**
1 **clove garlic, minced**
¼ **cup finely shredded
    Parmesan cheese**

1. Prepare Basic Crepes; keep warm.

2. For filling, melt margarine or butter in a large skillet; add mushrooms, green onion, rosemary or thyme, lemon-pepper seasoning, and garlic. Cook over medium heat until mushrooms and onion are tender and liquid has evaporated. Stir in *2 tablespoons* of the Parmesan cheese.

3. To serve, spoon some of the filling down the center of each crepe; roll up jelly-roll style. Serve immediately or keep warm in a 300° oven for up to 30 minutes. Just before serving, sprinkle with remaining Parmesan cheese. Makes 4 servings.

Nutrition Facts per serving: 84 calories, 5 g total fat (1 g saturated fat), 36 mg cholesterol, 149 mg sodium, 7 g carbohydrates, 0 g fiber, 4 g protein
Daily Values: 7% vit. A, 3% vit. C, 5% calcium, 5% iron

Brie Pancake

For your next party, cut this puff pancake into bite-size wedges for a great appetizer.

Prep: 10 minutes
Bake: 15 minutes
Oven: 425°
Makes 4 to 6 servings

 3 eggs
¾ cup milk
¾ cup all-purpose flour
½ of a 4½-ounce Brie cheese
    round, cut up
 2 tablespoons finely chopped
    green onion
 1 tablespoon margarine
    or butter
 2 ounces prosciutto or fully
    cooked ham, thinly sliced
   Melon wedges (optional)

1. In a food processor bowl or blender container combine eggs, milk, flour, and Brie. Cover and process or blend until nearly smooth. Stir in the green onion.

2. Heat a 10-inch ovenproof skillet or a 9×1½-inch round baking pan in a 425° oven for 2 minutes. Add margarine or butter; swirl to coat pan. Pour batter into hot skillet or pan. Bake pancake in the 425° oven for 15 to 20 minutes or until puffed and golden.

3. To serve, remove pancake from oven. Cut into wedges. Serve with slices of prosciutto or ham. If desired, serve with melon wedges. Pancake will collapse as it cools. Makes 4 to 6 servings.

Nutrition Facts per serving: 188 calories, 10 g total fat (3 g saturated fat), 119 mg cholesterol, 303 mg sodium, 13 g carbohydrates, 0 g fiber, 10 g protein **Daily Values:** 11% vit. A, 1% vit. C, 6% calcium, 7% iron

Prosciutto

*O*riginally from Italy, prosciutto is ham that has been seasoned and air-dried, not smoked as American ham is. The result is a somewhat sweetly spiced, rose-colored meat with a sheen. Prosciutto typically is very thinly sliced. It dries out quickly and should be used within a day or frozen for longer storage.

Wild Rice Pancakes

Wild Rice Pancakes

Loaded with the nutty taste of wild rice, these crunchy pancakes make a wonderful accompaniment to a main course of pork roast or baked chicken.

Prep: 20 minutes
Makes 16 pancakes

½ cup all-purpose flour
2 teaspoons sugar
¼ teaspoon salt
½ cup chopped fresh
    mushrooms
¼ cup chopped green onion
¼ cup finely chopped celery
1 tablespoon snipped fresh
    sage or ½ teaspoon dried
    sage, crushed
1 tablespoon cooking oil
1 cup low-fat ricotta cheese
3 egg yolks
¼ cup milk
1½ cups cooked wild rice
3 egg whites

1. Combine flour, sugar, and salt; set aside. In a small skillet cook mushrooms, green onion, celery, and sage in hot oil about 5 minutes or until vegetables are crisp-tender; cool slightly. Combine ricotta cheese, egg yolks, and milk; add vegetable mixture and cooked wild rice. Add rice mixture to flour mixture. Stir just until combined but still slightly lumpy.

2. In a medium mixing bowl beat egg whites with an electric mixer on medium to high speed until stiff peaks form (tips stand straight). Gently fold about one-fourth of the beaten whites into the batter to lighten; fold in remaining whites, leaving in a few puffs of egg white. Do not overbeat.

3. Heat a lightly greased griddle or heavy skillet over medium heat until a few drops of water dance across the surface. For each pancake, pour about 3 tablespoons batter onto the hot griddle. Spread batter into a circle about 2½ inches in diameter.

4. Cook over medium heat until pancakes are golden brown, turning to cook second sides when pancake surfaces are bubbly and edges are slightly dry (1 to 2 minutes per side). Serve immediately or keep warm in a loosely covered ovenproof dish in a 300° oven. Makes 16 pancakes.

Nutrition Facts per pancake: 68 calories, 2 g total fat (0 g saturated fat), 43 mg cholesterol, 59 mg sodium, 8 g carbohydrates, 0 g fiber, 4 g protein
Daily Values: 7% vit. A, 0% vit. C, 2% calcium, 2% iron

Wild Rice

Not a grain at all, wild rice is a marsh grass. It has a nutlike flavor and chewy texture. Before cooking, use a colander to wash wild rice thoroughly. For 1½ cups cooked rice, add ⅔ cup wild rice to 1⅓ cups boiling water. Cook, covered, 40 minutes or until most of the water is absorbed. Drain, if necessary.

Vegetable-Stuffed Puff Pancake

Enjoy this filled pancake for lunch or a light supper.

Prep: 10 minutes
Bake: 18 minutes
Oven: 450°
Makes 4 servings

½ cup all-purpose flour
½ cup milk
2 eggs
⅛ teaspoon salt
1 tablespoon cooking oil
    Nonstick spray coating
2 cups sliced fresh mushrooms
1 cup sliced onion (1 large)
1 cup coarsely shredded
    carrots
1 tablespoon water
1 10-ounce package frozen
    chopped spinach, thawed
    and well drained
1 8-ounce can tomato sauce
2 tablespoons snipped fresh
    basil or ½ teaspoon dried
    basil, crushed
1 cup crumbled feta cheese
    (4 ounces)
¼ cup sliced pitted ripe olives
    (optional)
1 tablespoon snipped fresh
    basil or parsley (optional)

1. In a mixing bowl combine flour, milk, eggs, and salt; beat until smooth.

2. Heat a 10-inch ovenproof skillet or a 9×1½-inch round baking pan in a 450° oven for 2 minutes. Carefully add cooking oil; swirl to coat skillet. Pour batter into hot skillet. Bake pancake in the 450° oven for 18 to 20 minutes or until puffed and golden.

3. Meanwhile, spray a large nonstick skillet with nonstick coating. Add mushrooms, onion, carrots, and water to skillet. Cook, covered, over medium heat about 5 minutes or until vegetables are tender, stirring often. Stir in spinach, tomato sauce, and the 2 tablespoons basil. Cook, uncovered, over medium heat about 4 minutes more or until slightly thickened, stirring often.

4. To serve, remove pancake from oven. Sprinkle ½ *cup* of the feta cheese over the pancake. Spoon vegetable mixture over cheese. Sprinkle with remaining ½ cup feta cheese and, if desired, the olives and the 1 tablespoon basil or parsley. Cut into wedges. Pancake will collapse as it cools. Makes 4 servings.

Nutrition Facts per serving: 276 calories, 13 g total fat (6 g saturated fat), 134 mg cholesterol, 845 mg sodium, 28 g carbohydrates, 3 g fiber, 13 g protein
Daily Values: 124% vit. A, 30% vit. C, 24% calcium, 22% iron

Basic Crepes

If you have an inverted crepe maker, follow the manufacturer's directions for cooking the crepes.

Prep: 10 minutes
Makes 20 crepes

3 eggs, slightly beaten
1⅓ cups milk
2 tablespoons margarine
   or butter, melted
¼ teaspoon salt
1 cup all-purpose flour
   Nonstick spray coating

1. In a medium mixing bowl combine eggs, milk, melted margarine or butter, and salt. Add flour. Beat with a rotary beater or electric mixer until smooth.

2. Spray a 6-inch nonstick skillet with nonstick coating. Heat skillet over medium heat until a few drops of water dance across the surface. Remove skillet from heat.

3. For each crepe, pour about 2 tablespoons batter into the hot skillet. Quickly lift and tilt skillet to spread batter into a thin, even circle. Cook about 1 minute or until top is set and edges are lightly browned. Gently loosen crepe with a narrow metal spatula; invert skillet to remove crepe.

4. Keep crepes warm in a loosely covered ovenproof dish in a 300° oven until ready to be filled, or cool crepes completely and freeze (see tip, right). Makes 20 crepes.

Nutrition Facts per crepe: 50 calories, 2 g total fat (1 g saturated fat), 33 mg cholesterol, 58 mg sodium, 5 g carbohydrates, 0 g fiber, 2 g protein
Daily Values: 3% vit. A, 0% vit. C, 2% calcium, 2% iron

Freezing Crepes

If your recipe calls for crepes, you can make them ahead and freeze them to cut down on preparation time later. To freeze, stack these paper-thin pancakes between 2 sheets of waxed paper. Place the stack in a moisture- and vaporproof freezer bag and freeze until you are ready to use them (no longer than 3 months). Let the crepes thaw at room temperature for about an hour before separating them to avoid tearing them.

Cheese Pancake Supreme

Prep: 30 minutes
Bake: 20 minutes
Oven: 400°
Makes 6 to 8 servings

Gjetost cheese lends a sweet caramel-like flavor to this treat. If you like, stir the batter together before dinner and chill it for up to 2 hours before baking for a warm and delightful dessert.

⅓ cup all-purpose flour
½ teaspoon baking powder
⅛ teaspoon salt
4 egg whites
½ cup sugar
4 egg yolks
⅓ cup milk
2 cups finely chopped, peeled apples
¾ cup shredded gjetost cheese or cheddar cheese (3 ounces)
1 tablespoon lemon juice
½ teaspoon ground cinnamon
1 recipe Sweetened Whipped Cream (see below) (optional)

1. Grease a 10-inch ovenproof skillet that has flared sides or a 2-quart rectangular baking dish; set aside.

2. Combine flour, baking powder, and salt. In a medium mixing bowl beat egg whites with an electric mixer on medium to high speed until soft peaks form (tips curl). Gradually beat in ⅓ *cup* of the sugar, 1 tablespoon at a time; beat until stiff peaks form (tips stand straight).

3. In a large mixing bowl beat egg yolks until combined. Alternately stir flour mixture and milk into beaten egg yolks. Stir in chopped apple, shredded cheese, and lemon juice. Gently fold beaten egg whites into batter, leaving in a few puffs of egg white. Do not overbeat. Pour batter into prepared skillet or baking dish; spread to edges. Combine remaining sugar and cinnamon; sprinkle over batter.

4. Bake in a 400° oven for 20 to 25 minutes or until a knife inserted near center comes out clean. To serve, cut into wedges or squares. If desired, top with Sweetened Whipped Cream. Serves 6 to 8.

Sweetened Whipped Cream: In a chilled bowl beat ½ cup *whipping cream*, 1 tablespoon *powdered sugar*, and ¼ teaspoon *vanilla* with chilled beaters of an electric mixer on medium to high speed just until soft peaks form. Chill until ready to use.

Nutrition Facts per serving: 238 calories, 8 g total fat (4 g saturated fat), 143 mg cholesterol, 209 mg sodium, 36 g carbohydrates, 1 g fiber, 7 g protein
Daily Values: 22% vit. A, 5% vit. C, 10% calcium, 5% iron

Cheese Pancake Supreme

Pancakes à la Mode

Prep: 15 minutes
Makes 6 servings

Spoon a bit of your favorite chocolate sauce over the ice cream for a banana split pancake.

1½ cups all-purpose flour
2 tablespoons sugar
2 teaspoons baking powder
½ teaspoon salt
½ teaspoon ground nutmeg
1½ cups milk
1 egg, slightly beaten
3 tablespoons cooking oil
1 banana, finely chopped
   (½ cup)
1 small apple, peeled and
   finely chopped (½ cup)
1 pint strawberry or vanilla
   ice cream
2 10-ounce packages frozen
   sliced strawberries, thawed

1. In a large mixing bowl combine flour, sugar, baking powder, salt, and nutmeg. In medium mixing bowl combine milk, egg, oil, banana, and apple. Stir just until combined but still slightly lumpy.

2. Heat a lightly greased griddle or heavy skillet over medium heat until a few drops of water dance across the surface. For each pancake, pour about ¼ cup batter onto the hot griddle. Spread batter into a circle about 4 inches in diameter.

3. Cook over medium heat until pancakes are golden brown, turning to cook second sides when pancake surfaces are bubbly and edges are slightly dry (about 1 to 2 minutes per side). Keep warm in a loosely covered ovenproof dish in a 300° oven. Repeat with remaining batter to make 12 pancakes.

4. To serve, place 2 pancakes on a dessert plate. Top with some of the ice cream and strawberries. Repeat with remaining pancakes, ice cream, and strawberries. Makes 6 servings.

Nutrition Facts per serving: 218 calories, 7 g total fat (3 g saturated fat), 30 mg cholesterol, 189 mg sodium, 36 g carbohydrates, 4 g fiber, 4 g protein
Daily Values: 5% vit. A, 35% vit. C, 11% calcium, 7% iron

Freeze Leftover Pancakes

When you have too many pancakes for one meal, wrap the extras up and store them in the freezer so you can have hot pancakes on those mornings when time is short.

To freeze pancakes, stack them with a piece of waxed paper between each layer. Overwrap the stack in a freezer bag, then place in a freezer container. Freeze for up to 4 months.

When you're ready to reheat them, stack the pancakes on a microwave-safe plate. Heat, uncovered, on high power until warm. Allow 40 to 45 seconds for 1 or 2 pancakes and 60 to 90 seconds for 3 or 4 pancakes.

Chocolate Fudge Pancakes

1¾ cups all-purpose flour
¾ teaspoon baking soda
½ teaspoon salt
1¾ cups buttermilk
¾ cup chocolate-flavored syrup
1 egg, slightly beaten
1 tablespoon margarine or
   butter, melted
1 teaspoon vanilla
½ cup chopped walnuts
   (optional)
¼ cup miniature semisweet
   chocolate pieces
1 recipe Chocolate Whipped
   Cream (see below)
   (optional)
Chocolate-flavored sprinkles
   (optional)

Prep: 15 minutes
Makes 20 pancakes

1. In a mixing bowl combine flour, baking soda, and salt. In another mixing bowl combine buttermilk, chocolate-flavored syrup, egg, margarine or butter, and vanilla. Add to flour mixture. Stir just until combined but slightly lumpy. If desired, stir in walnuts. Stir in miniature chocolate pieces.

2. Heat a lightly greased griddle or heavy skillet over medium heat until a few drops of water dance across the surface. For each pancake, pour about ¼ cup batter onto the hot griddle. Spread batter into a circle about 4 inches in diameter.

3. Cook over medium-low heat until pancakes are golden brown, turning to cook second sides when pancake surfaces are bubbly and edges are slightly dry (about 2 to 3 minutes per side).

4. Serve immediately or keep warm in a loosely covered ovenproof dish in a 300° oven. If desired, serve with Chocolate Whipped Cream and garnish with chocolate-flavored sprinkles. Makes 20 pancakes.

Chocolate Whipped Cream: In a chilled mixing bowl beat 1 cup *whipping cream*, 2 tablespoons *powdered sugar*, 2 tablespoons *unsweetened cocoa powder*, and ½ teaspoon *vanilla* with chilled beaters of an electric mixer on medium to high speed just until soft peaks form. Chill until ready to use.

Nutrition Facts per pancake: 90 calories, 2 g total fat (0 g saturated fat), 11 mg cholesterol, 139 mg sodium, 17 g carbohydrates, 0 g fiber, 2 g protein
Daily Values: 1% vit. A, 0% vit. C, 2% calcium, 4% iron

Sweet Cottage Cheese Crepes

Sweet Cottage Cheese Crepes

*Top these delicate, lemony crepes simply, with either a few fresh
berries or a sprinkle of powdered sugar.*

Prep: 45 minutes
Bake: 20 minutes
Oven: 350°
Makes 8 servings

Nonstick spray coating
2 cups **small-curd cottage cheese**
½ cup **dairy sour cream**
1 **egg yolk, slightly beaten**
2 tablespoons **granulated sugar**
2 teaspoons **finely shredded lemon peel**
1 cup **all-purpose flour**
2 tablespoons **sugar**
1½ cups **milk**
2 **eggs, slightly beaten**
1 tablespoon **margarine or butter, melted**
Sifted powdered sugar

1. Spray a 3-quart rectangular baking dish with nonstick coating; set aside. For filling, place cottage cheese in a blender container. Cover and blend until smooth. Transfer to a mixing bowl; stir in sour cream, egg yolk, 2 tablespoons sugar, and lemon peel. Beat with a wire whisk until combined. Set filling aside.

2. For crepes, in a medium mixing bowl combine flour, 2 tablespoons granulated sugar, milk, eggs, and melted margarine or butter. Beat with a wire whisk until smooth. Heat a lightly greased 6-inch skillet over medium heat until a few drops of water dance across the surface. Remove skillet from heat.

3. For each crepe, pour about 2 tablespoons batter into the hot skillet. Quickly lift and tilt skillet to spread batter in a thin, even circle. Cook about 1 minute or until top is set and edge is lightly browned. Loosen crepe; invert skillet to remove crepe. Repeat with remaining batter to make 16 crepes.

4. To assemble, spread unbrowned side of each crepe with a generous tablespoon of filling. Fold crepes in half, then fold in half again, forming a triangle. Place in a single layer in prepared baking dish. Bake in a 350° oven for 20 to 25 minutes or until heated through. Serve immediately, sprinkled with powdered sugar. Makes 8 servings.

Nutrition Facts per serving: 113 calories, 5 g total fat (2 g saturated fat), 49 mg cholesterol, 138 mg sodium, 111 g carbohydrates, 0 g fiber, 6 g protein
Daily Values: 8% vit. A, 1% vit. C, 4% calcium, 3% iron

French Silk Crepe Torte

You'll find a burst of color and flavor here as a chocolate filling teams with a bright red cherry topping. Best of all, this decadent torte can be made the day before.

Prep: 45 minutes
Chill: 5 to 24 hours
Makes 12 servings

Using Egg Substitutes

*I*f you like, you can replace whole eggs or egg yolks in any of our pancake recipes with a frozen or refrigerated egg substitute. Use ¼ cup egg substitute for 1 whole egg and 2 tablespoons egg substitute for 1 egg yolk.

Crepes
¾ cup all-purpose flour
2 tablespoons sugar
1 teaspoon baking powder
½ teaspoon salt
2 eggs, slightly beaten
⅔ cup milk
⅓ cup water
½ teaspoon vanilla

Filling
¾ cup sugar
¾ cup margarine or butter
1 6-ounce package (1 cup) semisweet chocolate pieces, melted and cooled
1 teaspoon vanilla
¾ cup refrigerated or frozen egg product, thawed

1 cup Cherry and Pineapple Topping (see page 109)

1. For crepes, in a mixing bowl combine flour, the 2 tablespoons sugar, baking powder, and salt. In another mixing bowl beat eggs, milk, water, and the ½ teaspoon vanilla until well combined. Add to flour mixture, beating until batter is smooth.

2. Heat a lightly greased 8-inch skillet over medium heat until a few drops of water dance across the surface. Remove skillet from heat. For each crepe, pour a scant 3 tablespoons batter into the hot skillet. Quickly lift and tilt the skillet to spread batter into a thin, even circle. Cook about 1 minute or until top is set and edge is lightly browned. Loosen crepe; invert skillet to remove crepe. Repeat with remaining batter, greasing skillet occasionally, to make 9 crepes.

3. For filling, in a large mixing bowl beat the ¾ cup sugar and margarine or butter with an electric mixer on medium speed about 4 minutes or until fluffy. Stir in cooled chocolate and the 1 teaspoon vanilla. Gradually add egg product, beating on high speed and scraping bowl constantly until light and fluffy.

4. To assemble, place a crepe on a serving plate. Spread a scant ½ cup filling over the crepe. Layer remaining crepes and filling, ending with a crepe. Cover; chill 5 to 24 hours. To serve, top torte with Cherry and Pineapple Topping. Makes 12 servings.

Nutrition Facts per serving: 320 calories, 17 g total fat (3 g saturated fat), 37 mg cholesterol, 301 mg sodium, 40 g carbohydrates, 0 g fiber, 5 g protein
Daily Values: 20% vit. A, 2% vit. C, 5% calcium, 8% iron

Carrot Cakes

Layer these carrot-filled pancakes with cream cheese frosting for a simple dessert that tastes like carrot cake.

Prep: 25 minutes
Makes 4 servings

1½ cups Buttermilk Pancake
    Mix (see page 80)
  3 tablespoons sugar
  ½ teaspoon ground cinnamon
  1 egg, slightly beaten
  1 cup water
  2 tablespoons cooking oil
  ¾ cup finely shredded carrots
  1 recipe Cream Cheese Spread
    (see below)
  ¼ cup chopped pecans or
    walnuts

1. In a bowl combine Buttermilk Pancake Mix, sugar, and cinnamon. In another bowl beat egg, water, and oil. Add to dry ingredients. Stir until well combined. Stir in carrots (batter will be thin).

2. Heat a lightly greased griddle or heavy skillet over medium heat until a few drops of water dance across the surface. For each pancake, pour about ¼ cup batter onto hot griddle. (Stir batter frequently to keep carrots well distributed.) Cook over medium heat until pancakes are golden brown, turning to cook second sides when pancake surfaces are bubbly and edges are slightly dry (about 1 to 2 minutes per side). Keep warm in a loosely covered ovenproof dish in a 300° oven. Repeat with remaining batter to make 12 pancakes.

3. To serve, spread 4 of the pancakes with a thin layer of Cream Cheese Spread (about 2 teaspoons). Stack pancakes and top with additional Cream Cheese Spread and 1 tablespoon of the nuts. Repeat with remaining pancakes, Cream Cheese Spread, and nuts. Makes 4 servings.

Cream Cheese Spread: Beat one 3-ounce package softened *cream cheese* and 2 tablespoons softened *margarine or butter* until fluffy. Add ½ cup sifted *powdered sugar* and ½ teaspoon *vanilla*. Beat until smooth and fluffy. Makes about ⅔ cup.

Nutrition Facts per serving: 330 calories, 13 g total fat (2 g saturated fat), 59 mg cholesterol, 485 mg sodium, 45 g carbohydrates, 2 g fiber, 8 g protein
Daily Values: 61% vit. A, 4% vit. C, 17% calcium, 14% iron

Rolled Candy Bar Pancakes

Choose your favorite candy bar to roll inside these cream-filled cakes.

Prep: 20 minutes
Makes 10 pancakes

1 cup whipping cream
2 tablespoons sugar
½ teaspoon vanilla
⅓ cup finely chopped
    chocolate-covered
    English toffee bar or
    other candy bar
1 egg, slightly beaten
⅔ cup milk
1 tablespoon margarine
    or butter, melted, or
    cooking oil
¾ cup Buttermilk Pancake
    Mix (see page 80)

1. In a chilled medium mixing bowl beat whipping cream, *1 tablespoon* of the sugar, and vanilla with chilled beaters of an electric mixer on medium to high speed just until soft peaks form. Fold in *3 tablespoons* of the chopped candy bar. Refrigerate whipped cream mixture while preparing pancakes.

2. For pancakes, in a mixing bowl beat egg, milk, and margarine or butter. Add the remaining 1 tablespoon sugar and the Buttermilk Pancake Mix. Stir just until combined but still slightly lumpy.

3. Heat a lightly greased griddle or heavy skillet over medium heat until a few drops of water dance across the surface. For each pancake, pour a scant 2 tablespoons batter onto the hot griddle (batter will flow into a circle about 4 inches in diameter).

4. Cook over medium heat until pancakes are golden brown, turning to cook second sides when pancake surfaces are bubbly and edges are slightly dry (about 1 to 2 minutes per side). Keep warm in a loosely covered ovenproof dish in a 300° oven.

5. To serve, spread each pancake with a rounded tablespoon of the whipped cream mixture; roll up. Place seam side down on a serving plate. Top with remaining whipped cream mixture. Sprinkle with remaining chopped candy. Makes 10 pancakes.

Nutrition Facts per pancake: 180 calories, 13 g total fat (6 g saturated fat), 58 mg cholesterol, 152 mg sodium, 14 g carbohydrates, 0 g fiber, 3 g protein
Daily Values: 14% vit. A, 0% vit. C, 6% calcium, 2% iron

Whipping Cream

You'll get the most volume from whipping cream if you whip it when it's extremely cold. For best results, chill the mixing bowl and beaters in the refrigerator about 15 minutes before using them to whip the cream.

Silver Dollar Pancakes

Bite-size and full of banana, these tiny pancakes are perfect for little fingers to grab.

Prep: 10 minutes
Makes 24 pancakes

½ cup all-purpose flour
1 tablespoon granulated sugar
1 teaspoon baking powder
¼ teaspoon salt
¼ teaspoon ground cinnamon
½ cup milk
1 egg, slightly beaten
½ cup mashed ripe banana
   Sifted powdered sugar or
    1 recipe Brown Sugar
    Syrup (see page 97)
    (optional)

1. In a mixing bowl combine flour, granulated sugar, baking powder, salt, and cinnamon. In another mixing bowl combine milk, egg, and banana. Add to flour mixture. Stir just until combined but still slightly lumpy.

2. Heat a lightly greased griddle or heavy skillet over medium heat until a few drops of water dance across the surface. For each pancake, spoon a scant 1 tablespoon batter onto the hot griddle.

3. Cook over medium heat until pancakes are golden brown, turning to cook the second sides when pancake surfaces are bubbly and edges are slightly dry (about ½ to 1 minute per side).

4. Serve immediately or keep warm in a loosely covered ovenproof dish in a 300° oven. If desired, serve with powdered sugar or Brown Sugar Syrup. Makes 24 pancakes (6 servings).

Nutrition Facts per serving: 126 calories, 2 g total fat (1 g saturated fat), 56 mg cholesterol, 256 mg sodium, 23 g carbohydrates, 1 g fiber, 4 g protein
Daily Values: 4% vit. A, 4% vit. C, 11% calcium, 7% iron

Rocky Road Pancakes

Prep: 15 minutes
Makes 16 pancakes

The cakelike texture of these pancakes begs for a sprinkling of miniature marshmallows and a drizzle of warm, hot fudge sauce. They're sure to be a hit with the chocolate lovers in your family.

2 cups Buttermilk Pancake Mix (see page 80)
1⅓ cups milk
2 eggs, slightly beaten
2 tablespoons sugar
2 tablespoons margarine or butter, melted
2 envelopes (2 ounces) premelted unsweetened chocolate or 2 ounces unsweetened chocolate, melted
½ cup semisweet chocolate pieces
½ cup chopped walnuts or pecans
2 cups miniature marshmallows
1 to 2 cups hot fudge ice-cream topping
Chopped walnuts or pecans (optional)

1. In a large mixing bowl combine Buttermilk Pancake Mix, milk, eggs, sugar, and melted margarine or butter. Stir just until combined but still slightly lumpy. Stir in chocolate, chocolate pieces, and the ½ cup walnuts or pecans.

2. Heat a lightly greased griddle or heavy skillet over medium heat until a few drops of water dance across the surface. Reduce heat to medium-low. For each pancake, pour a scant ¼ cup batter onto the hot griddle. Spread batter into a circle about 4 inches in diameter.

3. Cook over medium-low heat until pancakes are golden brown, turning to cook second sides when pancake surfaces are bubbly and edges are slightly dry (about 1 to 2 minutes per side). Top with a few marshmallows after turning to cook second sides.

4. Serve immediately drizzled with hot fudge topping. If desired, sprinkle with additional nuts. Makes about 16 pancakes.

Nutrition Facts per pancake with marshmallows and topping:
240 calories, 11 g total fat (3 g saturated fat), 30 mg cholesterol, 204 mg sodium, 34 g carbohydrates, 1 g fiber, 6 g protein
Daily Values: 5% vit. A, 0% vit. C, 10% calcium, 9% iron

Rocky Road Pancakes

Funny Face Pancakes

With a pancake "canvas" and a variety of toppings, there's no limit to your young artists' creative talents.

Prep: 10 minutes
Makes 16 pancakes

1 cup Buttermilk Pancake
  Mix (see page 80)
1 cup milk
1 egg, slightly beaten
1 tablespoon cooking oil
  Banana slices
  Canned peach slices
  Raisins
  Shredded coconut

1. In a medium mixing bowl combine Buttermilk Pancake Mix, milk, egg, and oil. Stir just until combined but still slightly lumpy.

2. Heat a lightly greased griddle or heavy skillet over medium heat until a few drops of water dance across the surface. For each pancake, pour about ¼ cup batter onto the hot griddle. Spread batter into a circle about 4 inches in diameter.

3. Cook over medium heat until pancakes are golden brown, turning to cook second sides when pancake surfaces are bubbly and edges are slightly dry (about 2 to 3 minutes per side).

4. Let youngsters make their own funny faces on the cooked pancakes, using their imaginations and bananas for eyes, peaches for eyebrows and mouths, raisins for noses and mouths, and coconut for whiskers. Serve warm. Makes 16 pancakes.

Nutrition Facts per pancake: 72 calories, 2 g total fat (1 g saturated fat), 15 mg cholesterol, 94 mg sodium, 11 g carbohydrates, 1 g fiber, 2 g protein
Daily Values: 2% vit. A, 2% vit. C, 4% calcium, 2% iron

The Name Game

Use your favorite pancake batter and a plastic bag as a writing tool to spell out your child's initials or name. Fill the plastic bag with batter. Cut a hole in the corner of the bag and squeeze the batter out the hole. (The size of the hole you make will determine the size of the pancake letters.)

Peanut Butter and Banana Fold-Overs

2 cups milk
2 eggs, slightly beaten
½ cup chunky peanut butter
2 cups Buttermilk Pancake
   Mix (see page 80)
¼ cup margarine or butter,
   melted
4 medium bananas, halved
   lengthwise, then crosswise
1 recipe Grape Syrup
   (see page 96) (optional)

1. In a large mixing bowl beat milk, eggs, and peanut butter with a wire whisk or electric mixer on medium speed until well combined. Add Buttermilk Pancake Mix, stirring until smooth.

2. Heat a lightly greased griddle or heavy skillet over medium heat until a few drops of water dance across the surface. For each pancake, pour about ¼ cup batter onto the hot griddle. Spread batter into a circle about 6 inches in diameter.

3. Cook over medium heat until pancakes are golden brown, turning to cook the second sides when pancake surfaces are bubbly and edges are slightly dry (about 1 to 2 minutes per side).

4. To serve, brush undersides of warm pancakes with melted margarine or butter; fold each pancake over a banana piece. If desired, serve with Grape Syrup. Makes 16 pancakes.

Nutrition Facts per pancake: 177 calories, 8 g total fat (2 g saturated fat), 31 mg cholesterol, 249 mg sodium, 21 g carbohydrates, 1 g fiber, 6 g protein
Daily Values: 6% vit. A, 5% vit. C, 9% calcium, 5% iron

Prep: 15 minutes
Makes 16 pancakes

Breakfast Tacos

A pancake folded taco-style holds a yummy ham, cheese, and pineapple filling.

Prep: 15 minutes
Bake: 10 minutes
Oven: 350°
Makes 10 tacos

Nonstick spray coating
2 teaspoons margarine
  or butter
⅓ **cup chopped celery**
⅓ **cup chopped green sweet**
  pepper
1 cup shredded cheddar cheese
  (4 ounces)
1 cup diced fully cooked ham
1 8-ounce can crushed
  pineapple (juice pack),
  well drained, or ¾ cup
  finely chopped apple
1⅓ **cups Buttermilk Pancake**
  Mix (see page 80)
1 cup water
1 egg, slightly beaten

1. Lightly spray a shallow baking pan with nonstick coating; set aside. For filling, in a small nonstick skillet melt margarine or butter over medium heat. Cook celery and sweet pepper in hot margarine or butter until tender. Remove from heat. Stir in ¾ *cup* of the cheese, the ham, and pineapple or apple. Set filling aside.

2. In a medium mixing bowl combine Buttermilk Pancake Mix, water, and egg; stir until smooth.

3. Heat a lightly greased griddle or heavy skillet over medium-high heat until a few drops of water dance across the surface. For each pancake, pour about ¼ cup batter onto the hot griddle. Spread batter into a circle about 4 inches in diameter.

4. Cook over medium heat until pancakes are golden brown, turning to cook second sides when pancake surfaces are bubbly and edges are slightly dry (about 2 to 3 minutes per side).

5. Place about ¼ cup filling in the center of each cooked pancake. Bring up the sides of each pancake, and stand pancake shells upright in prepared baking pan. Bake in a 350° oven for 10 to 12 minutes or until heated through. Sprinkle with remaining ¼ cup cheese. Makes 10 pancake tacos.

Nutrition Facts per pancake taco: 154 calories, 6 g total fat (3 g saturated fat), 43 mg cholesterol, 422 mg sodium, 16 g carbohydrates, 1 g fiber, 9 g protein
Daily Values: 6% vit. A, 14% vit. C, 13% calcium, 6% iron

Breakfast Tacos

Peanut Butter Pancakes with Peanut Butter Syrup

Peanut Butter Pancakes

Spread grape jelly between two of these fluffy pancakes for a satisfying peanut butter and jelly breakfast sandwich.

Prep: 15 minutes
Makes 14 pancakes

1½ cups all-purpose flour
 1 tablespoon sugar
 2 teaspoons baking powder
 ¼ teaspoon salt
 2 eggs, slightly beaten
 ¾ cup chunky peanut butter
1½ cups milk
   Grape jelly (optional)
 1 recipe Peanut Butter Syrup
   (see page 98) (optional)

1. In a mixing bowl combine flour, sugar, baking powder, and salt. In another mixing bowl stir together eggs and peanut butter until thoroughly combined; gradually stir in milk until combined (mixture may appear stiff at first, but it will thin when all the milk has been added). Add peanut butter mixture to the flour mixture. Stir just until combined but still slightly lumpy.

2. Heat a lightly greased griddle or heavy skillet over medium heat until a few drops of water dance across the surface. For each pancake, pour about ¼ cup batter onto the hot griddle. Spread batter into a circle about 4 inches in diameter.

3. Cook over medium heat until pancakes are golden brown, turning to cook second sides when pancake surfaces are bubbly and edges are slightly dry (2 to 3 minutes per side).

4. Serve immediately or keep warm in a loosely covered ovenproof dish in a 300° oven. If desired, serve with grape jelly and Peanut Butter Syrup. Makes 14 pancakes.

Nutrition Facts per pancake: 154 calories, 8 g total fat (2 g saturated fat), 32 mg cholesterol, 179 mg sodium, 15 g carbohydrates, 1 g fiber, 6 g protein
Daily Values: 2% vit. A, 0% vit. C, 7% calcium, 6% iron

Chocolate Chip-Peanut Butter Pancakes: Prepare as above, except stir ½ cup *miniature semisweet chocolate pieces* into the batter.

Buttermilk Pancake Mix

Prep: 10 minutes
Makes 11 cups

8 cups all-purpose flour
2 cups buttermilk powder
½ cup sugar
2 tablespoons plus 2 teaspoons
  baking powder
4 teaspoons baking soda
2 teaspoons salt

1. In a large mixing bowl combine flour, buttermilk powder, sugar, baking powder, baking soda, and salt. Stir until well combined. Store in an airtight container for up to 6 weeks.

2. To use, spoon lightly into a measuring cup and level off with a straight-edged spatula. Makes 11 cups.

Nutrition Facts per ½ cup dry mix: 213 calories, 1 g total fat (0 g saturated fat), 8 mg cholesterol, 612 mg sodium, 42 g carbohydrates, 1 g fiber, 8 g protein
Daily Values: 0% vit. A, 1% vit. C, 21% calcium, 14% iron

Tips on Mixes

*H*omemade pancake mixes are simple to stir together and keep for at least several weeks. Before you get started fixing a mix, review these tips from our Test Kitchen.

- *Measure all ingredients accurately.*
- *Store the mix in an airtight container.*
- *Label and date the container, including the date it was made and the date by which it should be used.*
- *Keep the mix in a cool, dry place for up to 6 weeks. For longer storage, freeze it for up to 6 months. Allow the mix to come to room temperature before using.*
- *To measure, stir the mix, then lightly spoon it into a measuring cup. Do not pack down the mixture. Level off the cup with a straight-edged spatula.*

Buttermilk Pancakes

Prep: 10 minutes
Makes 16 pancakes

2 eggs, slightly beaten
1⅔ cups water
⅓ cup margarine or butter, melted, or cooking oil
2½ cups Buttermilk Pancake Mix (see page 80)
1 recipe Spicy Apple Topping (see page 108) (optional)

1. In a large mixing bowl combine eggs, water, and margarine or butter, or oil. Add Buttermilk Pancake Mix. Stir just until combined but still slightly lumpy.

2. Heat a lightly greased griddle or heavy skillet over medium heat until a few drops of water dance across the surface. For each pancake, pour about ¼ cup batter onto the hot griddle. Spread batter into a circle about 4 inches in diameter.

3. Cook over medium heat until pancakes are golden brown, turning to cook second sides when pancake surfaces are bubbly and edges are slightly dry (about 2 to 3 minutes per side).

4. Serve immediately or keep warm in a loosely covered ovenproof dish in a 300° oven. If desired, serve with Spicy Apple Topping. Makes 16 pancakes.

Nutrition Facts per pancake: 109 calories, 5 g total fat (1 g saturated fat), 29 mg cholesterol, 243 mg sodium, 13 g carbohydrates, 0 g fiber, 3 g protein
Daily Values: 6% vit. A, 0% vit. C, 7% calcium, 5% iron

Cornmeal Pancake Mix

Prep: 15 minutes
Makes 5½ cups

2¼ cups all-purpose flour
1¼ cups cornmeal
¾ cup buttermilk powder
4 teaspoons baking powder
2 teaspoons baking soda
½ teaspoon salt
¾ cup butter-flavored
shortening

1. Mix flour, cornmeal, buttermilk powder, baking powder, baking soda, and salt. Stir until well combined. Cut shortening into flour mixture until mixture resembles coarse crumbs. Store in an airtight container for up to 6 weeks. To use, spoon lightly into a measuring cup and level off with a straight-edged spatula. Makes 5½ cups.

Nutrition Facts per ½ cup dry mix: 299 calories, 15 g total fat (4 g saturated fat), 6 mg cholesterol, 501 mg sodium, 35 g carbohydrates, 1 g fiber, 7 g protein
Daily Values: 1% vit. A, 0% vit. C, 18% calcium, 13% iron

Orange-Cornmeal Pancakes

Prep: 10 minutes
Makes 12 pancakes

1 egg, slightly beaten
1¼ cups water
2 teaspoons finely shredded
orange peel
2 tablespoons cooking oil
2 cups Cornmeal Pancake Mix
(see above)
½ cup chopped walnuts
(optional)
1 recipe Citrus Syrup
(see page 98) (optional)
Fresh fruit such as chopped
nectarines or peaches,
sliced strawberries, and/or
sliced kiwifruit (optional)

1. In a mixing bowl combine egg, water, orange peel, and oil. Add Cornmeal Pancake Mix. Stir just until combined but still slightly lumpy. If desired, add nuts. Heat a lightly greased griddle or heavy skillet over medium heat until a few drops of water dance across the surface. For each pancake, pour about ¼ cup batter onto the hot griddle.

2. Cook over medium heat until pancakes are golden brown, turning to cook second sides when pancake surfaces are bubbly and edges are slightly dry (about 1 to 2 minutes per side). Serve immediately or keep warm in a loosely covered ovenproof dish in a 300° oven. If desired, serve with Citrus Syrup and fresh fruit. Makes 12 pancakes.

Nutrition Facts per pancake: 126 calories, 8 g total fat (2 g saturated fat), 20 mg cholesterol, 173 mg sodium, 12 g carbohydrates, 0 g fiber, 3 g protein
Daily Values: 1% vit. A, 1% vit. C, 6% calcium, 4% iron

Orange-Cornmeal Pancakes with Citrus Syrup

Whole Wheat Pancake Mix

Prep: 15 minutes
Makes 14 cups

4 cups whole wheat flour
4 cups all-purpose flour
1½ cups nonfat dry milk powder
¾ cup sugar
½ cup toasted wheat germ
3 tablespoons baking powder
2 teaspoons salt
1½ cups plain or butter-flavored shortening

1. In a large mixing bowl combine whole wheat flour, all-purpose flour, dry milk powder, sugar, wheat germ, baking powder, and salt. Stir until well combined. Use a pastry blender to cut the shortening into the flour mixture until mixture resembles coarse crumbs. Store in an airtight container for up to 6 weeks.

2. To use, spoon lightly into a measuring cup and level off with a straight-edged spatula. Makes 14 cups.

Nutrition Facts per ½ cup dry mix: 267 calories, 12 g total fat (3 g saturated fat), 1 mg cholesterol, 301 mg sodium, 35 g carbohydrates, 3 g fiber, 6 g protein
Daily Values: 2% vit. A, 0% vit. C, 14% calcium, 12% iron

Pancake Lore

Early English colonists in the New World found the Indians preparing soft batter cakes from cornmeal; they were called Indian cakes as early as 1607. Perhaps these were the pancakes colonists called Shawnee cakes and eventually renamed journey cakes. Dutch colonists made similar pancakes using buckwheat flour, which by 1740 were being called buckwheat cakes. By the middle of the 18th century, early Americans were making hoecakes—a version of corn pone baked on a hoe over an open fire.

Whole Wheat Pancakes

Serve these tummy-tempting hotcakes with Homemade Maple Syrup (see recipe, page 94).

Prep: 5 minutes
Makes 8 pancakes

1 egg, slightly beaten
1 cup water
2 cups Whole Wheat Pancake
   Mix (see page 84)

1. In a medium mixing bowl combine the egg and water. Add Whole Wheat Pancake Mix. Stir just until combined but still slightly lumpy.

2. Heat a lightly greased griddle or heavy skillet over medium heat until a few drops of water dance across the surface. For each pancake, pour about ¼ cup batter onto the hot griddle.

3. Cook over medium heat until pancakes are golden brown, turning to cook second sides when pancake surfaces are bubbly and edges are slightly dry (about 2 to 3 minutes per side).

4. Serve immediately or keep warm in a loosely covered ovenproof dish in a 300° oven. Makes 8 pancakes.

Nutrition Facts per pancake: 75 calories, 4 g total fat (1 g saturated fat), 27 mg cholesterol, 83 mg sodium, 9 g carbohydrates, 1 g fiber, 2 g protein
Daily Values: 1% vit. A, 0% vit. C, 3% calcium, 3% iron

Oatmeal Pancake Mix

Prep: 15 minutes
Makes 12 cups

For a spiced pancake mix, add 5 teaspoons of ground cinnamon to the dry mixture.

4 cups all-purpose flour
4 cups quick-cooking
    rolled oats
1½ cups nonfat dry milk powder
¼ cup baking powder
1½ teaspoons salt
1½ cups butter-flavored or plain
    shortening

1. In a large mixing bowl combine the flour, rolled oats, dry milk powder, baking powder, and salt. Stir until well combined. Use a pastry blender to cut shortening into flour mixture until mixture resembles coarse crumbs. Store in an airtight container for up to 6 weeks.

2. To use, spoon lightly into a measuring cup and level off with a straight-edged spatula. Makes 12 cups.

Nutrition Facts per ½ cup dry mix: 251 calories, 14 g total fat (3 g saturated fat), 1 mg cholesterol, 339 mg sodium, 26 g carbohydrates, 2 g fiber, 6 g protein
Daily Values: 3% vit. A, 0% vit. C, 19% calcium, 11% iron

Pancake Lore

Before the days of yeast and baking soda, early cooks used hardwood ashes to leaven their pancakes. They poured boiling water over sifted ashes in a cup, let the ashes settle, and used the liquid to make their pancakes rise.

Still other resourceful cooks depended on the winter weather for tenderness. Newly fallen snow contains a large proportion of ammonia. When used as part of the recipe's liquid (a teacup of snow to a pint of milk, according to some cook's notes), it makes cakes that are light and fluffy.

Oatmeal Pancakes

This simple batter looks thin when you first mix it, but don't be fooled. It thickens in a few minutes.

Prep: 5 minutes
Stand: 5 minutes
Makes 8 pancakes

**2 cups Oatmeal Pancake Mix
(see page 86)
1 cup water
1 egg, slightly beaten
1 recipe Caramel Apple Sauce
(see page 105) (optional)**

1. In a medium mixing bowl combine Oatmeal Pancake Mix, water, and egg. Stir just until moistened. Let stand 5 minutes to thicken slightly.

2. Heat a lightly greased griddle or heavy skillet over medium heat until a few drops of water dance across the surface. For each pancake, pour about ¼ cup batter onto the hot griddle.

3. Cook over medium heat until pancakes are golden brown, turning to cook second sides when pancake surfaces are bubbly and edges are slightly dry (about 2 to 3 minutes per side).

4. Serve immediately or keep warm in a loosely covered ovenproof dish in a 300° oven. If desired, serve with Caramel Apple Sauce. Makes 8 pancakes.

Nutrition Facts per pancake: 135 calories, 8 g total fat (2 g saturated fat), 27 mg cholesterol, 178 mg sodium, 13 g carbohydrates, 1 g fiber, 4 g protein
Daily Values: 2% vit. A, 0% vit. C, 9% calcium, 6% iron

Buckwheat Pancakes with Hot Cranberry Sauce

Buckwheat Pancake Mix

Prep: 10 minutes
Makes 5 cups

2½ cups stone-ground
    buckwheat flour
2½ cups whole wheat flour
  4 teaspoons baking powder
  4 teaspoons sugar
  2 teaspoons baking soda
  2 teaspoons salt

1. Mix buckwheat flour, whole wheat flour, baking powder, sugar, baking soda, and salt. Stir until well combined. Store in an airtight container for up to 6 weeks. To use, spoon into a measuring cup; level off with a straight-edged spatula. Makes 5 cups.

Nutrition Facts per ½ cup dry mix: 210 calories, 1 g total fat (0 g saturated fat), 0 mg cholesterol, 825 mg sodium, 45 g carbohydrates, 8 g fiber, 8 g protein
Daily Values: 0% vit. A, 0% vit. C, 13% calcium, 17% iron

Buckwheat Pancakes

Prep: 10 minutes
Makes 10 pancakes

1¼ cups buttermilk
  1 egg yolk
  2 tablespoons margarine or
    butter, melted
  1 cup Buckwheat Pancake
    Mix (see above)
  1 egg white
  1 recipe Hot Cranberry Sauce
    (see page 107) (optional)

1. In a mixing bowl combine buttermilk, egg yolk, and margarine or butter. Add Buckwheat Pancake Mix; stir just until combined but still slightly lumpy. Beat egg white with an electric mixer on medium to high speed until stiff peaks form (tips stand straight). Gently fold beaten white into flour mixture, leaving in a few puffs of egg white. Do not overbeat. Heat a lightly greased griddle or heavy skillet over medium heat until a few drops of water dance across the surface. For each pancake, pour about ¼ cup batter onto hot griddle. Cook over medium heat until pancakes are golden brown, turning to cook second sides when pancake surfaces are bubbly and edges are slightly dry (about 1½ to 2 minutes per side). Serve immediately or keep warm in a loosely covered ovenproof dish in a 300° oven. If desired, serve with Hot Cranberry Sauce. Makes 10 pancakes.

Nutrition Facts per pancake: 91 calories, 4 g total fat (1 g saturated fat), 25 mg cholesterol, 256 mg sodium, 12 g carbohydrates, 2 g fiber, 4 g protein
Daily Values: 7% vit. A, 0% vit. C, 6% calcium, 4% iron

Four-Grain Pancake Mix

Prep: 10 minutes
Makes 5 cups

1½ cups all-purpose flour
1 cup rye flour
1 cup whole wheat flour
1 cup yellow cornmeal
2 tablespoons baking powder
1 teaspoon baking soda
½ teaspoon salt

1. In a large mixing bowl combine all-purpose flour, rye flour, whole wheat flour, yellow cornmeal, baking powder, baking soda, and salt. Stir until well combined. Store in an airtight container for up to 6 weeks.

2. To use, spoon lightly into a measuring cup and level off with a straight-edged spatula. Makes 5 cups.

Nutrition Facts per ½ cup dry mix: 191 calories, 1 g total fat (0 g saturated fat), 0 mg cholesterol, 452 mg sodium, 41 g carbohydrates, 4 g fiber, 6 g protein
Daily Values: 0% vit. A, 0% vit. C, 17% calcium, 15% iron

Pancake Lore

Shrove Tuesday—the day before Ash Wednesday—is traditionally a day for eating pancakes. Legend has it that in 1445, a woman in Olney, Buckinghamshire, England, was making pancakes that holiday when she heard the church bells ring. Afraid she would miss the shriving service, she ran to church wearing her apron and carrying a skilletful of pancakes. In subsequent years, her run turned into an annual race.

Today, the annual International Pancake Race is run simultaneously by women in Liberal, Kansas, and in Olney. Both races start at 11:55 a.m. local time on Shrove Tuesday. Each contestant runs a 415-yard S-shaped course through the main streets of her town wearing a scarf on her head and an apron, and carrying a skillet with a pancake. The pancake must be flipped after the starting signal and again after crossing the finish line. The first to arrive at the church receives a kiss from the bell ringer and the blessing, "The peace of the Lord be always with you." The winning times in each town are compared and the international champion is proclaimed.

Four-Grain Pancakes

A spoonful of either Maple Butter (see recipe, page 101) or Strawberry Butter (see recipe, page 100) complements these golden pancakes.

Prep: 10 minutes
Makes 16 pancakes

2 eggs, slightly beaten
1⅓ cups buttermilk
2 tablespoons margarine or butter, melted
1½ cups Four-Grain Pancake Mix (see page 90)

1. In a mixing bowl combine eggs, buttermilk, and margarine or butter. Add Four-Grain Pancake Mix. Stir just until combined but still slightly lumpy.

2. Heat a lightly greased griddle or heavy skillet over medium heat until a few drops of water dance across the surface. For each pancake, pour about ¼ cup batter onto the hot griddle. Spread batter into a circle about 4 inches in diameter.

3. Cook over medium heat until pancakes are golden brown, turning to cook second sides when pancake surfaces are bubbly and edges are slightly dry (about 2 to 3 minutes per side).

4. Serve immediately or keep warm in a loosely covered ovenproof dish in a 300° oven. Makes about 16 pancakes.

Nutrition Facts per pancake: 88 calories, 3 g total fat (1 g saturated fat), 37 mg cholesterol, 174 mg sodium, 12 g carbohydrates, 1 g fiber, 3 g protein
Daily Values: 4% vit. A, 0% vit. C, 7% calcium, 4% iron

All Margarines Are Not Created Equal

*T*here are many low-fat and reduced-calorie margarines and spreads available today. For cooking and baking, our Test Kitchen suggests using a margarine that contains no less than 60 percent vegetable oil. Do not use stick or tub products labeled "spreads." These products contain a high ratio of water to vegetable oil, making them unsuitable for many recipes.

Whole-Grain Pancake Mix

At your supermarket, look for wheat bran, sometimes labeled Miller's bran, with the other flours.

Prep: 15 minutes
Makes 12 cups

4 cups whole wheat flour
2 cups all-purpose flour
1 cup toasted wheat germ
1 cup wheat bran
1 cup buttermilk powder
2 tablespoons baking powder
2 teaspoons salt
1 teaspoon baking soda
1½ cups plain or butter-flavored shortening

1. In a large mixing bowl combine whole wheat flour, all-purpose flour, wheat germ, wheat bran, buttermilk powder, baking powder, salt, and baking soda. Stir until well combined.

2. Use a pastry blender to cut shortening into flour mixture until mixture resembles coarse crumbs. Store in an airtight container in the refrigerator for up to 6 weeks.

3. To use, spoon lightly into a measuring cup and level off with a straight-edged spatula. Makes 12 cups.

Nutrition Facts per ½ cup dry mix: 268 calories, 15 g total fat (4 g saturated fat), 4 mg cholesterol, 363 mg sodium, 29 g carbohydrates, 4 g fiber, 7 g protein
Daily Values: 0% vit. A, 0% vit. C, 13% calcium, 14% iron

The Versatile Pancake

*P*ersonalize plain pancake batter by stirring in one of the following foods, or experiment with others that you like. The amounts suggested are for about 16 pancakes. (When time is at a premium, combine a favorite flavor with a purchased pancake mix for an extra-easy meal.)

- *¾ cup finely chopped meat, such as ham, chicken, or beef*
- *½ cup shredded cheese*
- *½ cup coconut*
- *½ cup mixed dried fruit bits*
- *½ cup chocolate chips*
- *1 to 2 teaspoons finely shredded orange or lemon peel*
- *½ teaspoon ground cinnamon*
- *¼ teaspoon ground nutmeg or allspice*

Whole-Grain Pancakes

Prep: 10 minutes

Makes 10 pancakes

¾ cup water
2 egg yolks
1⅔ cups **Whole-Grain Pancake Mix** (see page 92)
2 egg whites
1 recipe **Orange-Molasses Syrup** (see page 97) (optional)

1. In a large mixing bowl combine water and egg yolks. Add Whole-Grain Pancake Mix. Stir just until combined but still slightly lumpy.

2. In a small mixing bowl beat egg whites with an electric mixer on medium to high speed until stiff peaks form (tips stand straight). Gently fold beaten egg whites into batter, leaving in a few puffs of egg white. Do not overbeat.

3. Heat a lightly greased griddle or heavy skillet over medium heat until a few drops of water dance across the surface. For each pancake, pour about ¼ cup batter onto the hot griddle.

4. Cook over medium heat until pancakes are golden brown, turning to cook second sides when pancake surfaces are bubbly and edges are slightly dry (about 1 to 2 minutes per side).

5. Serve immediately or keep warm in a loosely covered ovenproof dish in a 300° oven. If desired, serve with Orange-Molasses Syrup. Makes 10 pancakes.

Nutrition Facts per pancake: 113 calories, 6 g total fat (2 g saturated fat), 49 mg cholesterol, 144 mg sodium, 11 g carbohydrates, 1 g fiber, 4 g protein
Daily Values: 7% vit. A, 0% vit. C, 5% calcium, 5% iron

Separating Eggs

*W*hen a recipe calls for separating the egg yolks from the whites, don't pass the yolk between shell halves. Use an egg separator instead.

Carefully crack open an egg into a small bowl or custard cup. Over another small bowl, pour the egg into an egg separator. When the white has drained from the yolk, place the egg yolk in a separate bowl.

Homemade Maple Syrup

Start to Finish:
10 minutes
Makes 2 cups

2 cups sugar
1 cup water
1 tablespoon maple flavoring

1. In a medium saucepan combine sugar and water. Bring to boiling over medium-high heat. Reduce heat and simmer, uncovered, for 5 minutes. Remove saucepan from heat and stir in maple flavoring. Serve warm or cool. (Mixture thickens somewhat upon cooling.) Cover and refrigerate remaining syrup for up to 1 week. Makes 2 cups.

Nutrition Facts per tablespoon: 50 calories, 0 g total fat (0 g saturated fat), 0 mg cholesterol, 0 mg sodium, 13 g carbohydrates, 0 g fiber, 0 g protein
Daily Values: 0% vit. A, 0% vit. C, 0% calcium, 0% iron

Blueberry Syrup

Prep: 5 minutes
Cook: 25 minutes
Makes 1 cup

This not-too-sweet syrup (see photo, page 27) is loaded with whole berries.

2 cups fresh or frozen blueberries
½ cup water
⅓ cup sugar
2 teaspoons lime juice or lemon juice

1. In a medium saucepan combine *1 cup* of the blueberries, the water, sugar, and lime or lemon juice. Cook and stir over medium heat for 2 to 3 minutes or until sugar dissolves. Bring to boiling. Reduce heat and simmer, uncovered, for 15 to 20 minutes or until slightly thickened, stirring occasionally.

2. Stir in the remaining 1 cup blueberries and cook, stirring occasionally, 2 to 3 minutes more or until blueberries become soft. Serve warm. Cover and refrigerate remaining syrup for up to 1 week. Makes 1 cup.

Nutrition Facts per tablespoon: 26 calories, 0 g total fat (0 g saturated fat), 0 mg cholesterol, 1 mg sodium, 7 g carbohydrates, 0 g fiber, 0 g protein
Daily Values: 0% vit. A, 4% vit. C, 0% calcium, 0% iron

Cider and Maple Syrup

Pair these harvest flavors with another fall favorite—Pumpkin Pancakes (see recipe, page 8).

Prep: 5 minutes
Cook: 20 minutes
Makes 1 cup

1 cup apple cider
1 cup maple-flavored syrup

1. In a small saucepan combine apple cider and syrup. Bring to boiling over medium heat. Simmer, uncovered, for 15 to 20 minutes or until thickened slightly (you should have about 1 cup of syrup). Serve warm. Cover and refrigerate remaining syrup for up to 1 week. Makes 1 cup.

Nutrition Facts per tablespoon: 58 calories, 0 g total fat (0 g saturated fat), 0 mg cholesterol, 2 mg sodium, 15 g carbohydrates, 0 g fiber, 0 g protein
Daily Values: 0% vit. A, 0% vit. C, 0% calcium, 2% iron

Spiced Syrup

Serve this cinnamon- and allspice-flavored syrup with Sweet Potato Pancakes (see recipe, page 41) or Oatmeal Pancakes (see recipe, page 87).

Start to Finish:
10 minutes
Makes 1 cup

1 cup maple-flavored syrup
2 tablespoons margarine
  or butter
½ teaspoon ground cinnamon
⅛ teaspoon ground allspice
  or nutmeg

1. In a small saucepan combine syrup, margarine or butter, cinnamon, and allspice or nutmeg. Bring to boiling over medium-high heat; boil for 2 minutes.

2. Remove from heat; beat with a wire whisk until well combined. Serve warm. Cover and refrigerate remaining syrup for up to 1 week. Makes 1 cup.

Nutrition Facts per tablespoon: 63 calories, 1 g total fat (0 g saturated fat), 0 mg cholesterol, 19 mg sodium, 13 g carbohydrates, 0 g fiber, 0 g protein
Daily Values: 1% vit. A, 0% vit. C, 0% calcium, 1% iron

Cranberry Syrup

Like pancakes, ice cream gets a flavor boost when topped with a few spoonfuls of this tangy syrup.

Prep: 5 minutes
Cook: 35 minutes
Makes 2 cups

2½ cups cranberry juice cocktail
¾ cup light-colored corn syrup
½ cup sugar

1. In a medium saucepan combine cranberry juice cocktail, corn syrup, and sugar. Stir to dissolve sugar. Bring to a rolling boil over medium-high heat. Boil about 30 minutes or until reduced to 2 cups. Do not stir during boiling. Serve warm. Cover and refrigerate remaining syrup for up to 1 week. Makes 2 cups.

Nutrition Facts per tablespoon: 46 calories, 0 g total fat (0 g saturated fat), 0 mg cholesterol, 6 mg sodium, 12 g carbohydrates, 0 g fiber, 0 g protein
Daily Values: 0% vit. A, 11% vit. C, 0% calcium, 2% iron

Grape Syrup

Start to Finish:
12 minutes
Makes 1¾ cups

1 cup grape jam or jelly
½ cup light-colored corn syrup
¼ cup water

1. In a small saucepan combine grape jam or jelly, corn syrup, and water. Cook and stir over medium-low heat until mixture is hot and jam or jelly melts. Do not boil. (If melted jam mixture isn't smooth after heating, beat with a wire whisk or rotary beater until combined.) Serve warm. Cover and refrigerate remaining syrup for up to 1 week. Makes 1¾ cups.

Nutrition Facts per tablespoon: 48 calories, 0 g total fat (0 g saturated fat), 0 mg cholesterol, 6 mg sodium, 12 g carbohydrates, 0 g fiber, 0 g protein
Daily Values: 0% vit. A, 0% vit. C, 0% calcium, 2% iron

Orange-Molasses Syrup

1 cup light molasses
5 or 6 thin orange slices,
   halved

1. In a small saucepan combine molasses and orange slices. Bring to boiling. Reduce heat and simmer, uncovered, for 5 minutes. Remove orange slices. Cool syrup slightly. Serve warm. Cover and refrigerate remaining syrup for up to 1 week. Makes 1 cup.

Prep: 5 minutes
Cook: 10 minutes
Makes 1 cup

Nutrition Facts per tablespoon: 52 calories, 0 g total fat (0 g saturated fat), 0 mg cholesterol, 3 mg sodium, 13 g carbohydrates, 0 g fiber, 0 g protein
Daily Values: 0% vit. A, 3% vit. C, 2% calcium, 6% iron

Brown Sugar Syrup

2 cups packed dark
   brown sugar
1 cup water
1 teaspoon vanilla

1. In a medium saucepan combine brown sugar and water. Cook and stir over medium-high heat until sugar dissolves. Bring to boiling. Reduce heat and simmer, uncovered, for 5 minutes. Remove from heat. Stir in vanilla. Serve warm or cool. Cover and refrigerate remaining syrup for up to 1 week. Makes 1⅔ cups.

Start to Finish:
  10 minutes
Makes 1⅔ cups

Nutrition Facts per tablespoon: 50 calories, 0 g total fat (0 g saturated fat), 0 mg cholesterol, 4 mg sodium, 13 g carbohydrates, 0 g fiber, 0 g protein
Daily Values: 0% vit. A, 0% vit. C, 0% calcium, 1% iron

Warming Syrup

Pancakes stay warm longer and taste better when served with warm syrup. Heat syrup in a microwave-safe container, uncovered, on high power until warm. Allow 30 to 60 seconds for ½ cup syrup and 1 to 1½ minutes for 1 cup syrup. Or, on the stovetop, heat syrup in a saucepan over medium-low heat until warm, stirring occasionally.

Peanut Butter Syrup

Start to Finish:
10 minutes
Makes 1½ cups

For double peanut pleasure, drizzle this syrup over Peanut Butter Pancakes (see recipe and photo, pages 78 and 79).

**3 tablespoons butter
   or margarine
⅓ cup creamy or chunky
   peanut butter
1 cup maple-flavored syrup
½ cup water**

1. In a medium saucepan melt the butter or margarine over low heat. Stir in peanut butter until smooth. Combine syrup and water; stir into peanut butter mixture. Bring to boiling over medium-high heat, stirring constantly. Reduce heat and simmer, uncovered, about 5 minutes more or until slightly thickened. Serve warm or cool. Cover and refrigerate remaining syrup for up to 1 week. (Store only 3 days if chunky peanut butter is used.) Makes 1½ cups.

Nutrition Facts per tablespoon: 67 calories, 3 g total fat (1 g saturated fat), 4 mg cholesterol, 33 mg sodium, 9 g carbohydrates, 0 g fiber, 1 g protein
Daily Values: 1% vit. A, 0% vit. C, 0% calcium, 1% iron

Citrus Syrup

Prep: 5 minutes
Cook: 20 minutes
Makes ¾ cup

Make variations of this refreshing syrup (see photo, page 83) by stirring in an 8-ounce can of drained pineapple tidbits or an 11-ounce can of drained mandarin orange sections.

**2 teaspoons finely shredded
   orange peel or lemon peel
1 cup orange juice
2 tablespoons lemon juice
½ cup sugar**

1. In a medium saucepan combine the orange peel or lemon peel, orange juice, lemon juice, and sugar. Bring to boiling over medium-high heat, stirring occasionally. Reduce heat and simmer, uncovered, about 15 minutes or until reduced to ¾ cup, stirring occasionally. Serve warm or cool. Cover and refrigerate remaining syrup for up to 1 week. Makes ¾ cup.

Nutrition Facts per tablespoon: 42 calories, 0 g total fat (0 g saturated fat), 0 mg cholesterol, 0 mg sodium, 11 g carbohydrates, 0 g fiber, 0 g protein
Daily Values: 0% vit. A, 19% vit. C, 0% calcium, 0% iron

Orange-Honey Butter

½ cup butter or margarine, softened
2 tablespoons honey
1 teaspoon finely shredded orange or lemon peel

1. In a small mixing bowl beat butter or margarine, honey, and orange peel with an electric mixer on medium speed until light and fluffy. Cover and refrigerate for up to 1 week. Serve at room temperature. Makes ¾ cup.

Nutrition Facts per teaspoon: 26 calories, 3 g total fat (2 g saturated fat), 7 mg cholesterol, 26 mg sodium, 1 g carbohydrates, 0 g fiber, 0 g protein
Daily Values: 2% vit. A, 0% vit. C, 0% calcium, 0% iron

Start to Finish:
5 minutes
Makes ¾ cup

Spiced Honey Butter

In addition to pancakes, enjoy this distinctive butter on toasted bagels, English muffins, or whole wheat toast.

½ cup butter or margarine, softened
¼ cup honey
½ teaspoon ground cinnamon

1. In a small mixing bowl beat butter or margarine, honey, and cinnamon with an electric mixer on medium speed until light and fluffy. Cover and refrigerate for up to 1 week. Serve at room temperature. Makes ¾ cup.

Nutrition Facts per teaspoon: 30 calories, 3 g total fat (2 g saturated fat), 7 mg cholesterol, 26 mg sodium, 2 g carbohydrates, 0 g fiber, 0 g protein
Daily Values: 2% vit. A, 0% vit. C, 0% calcium, 0% iron

Start to Finish:
5 minutes
Makes ¾ cup

Strawberry Butter

Extra-ripe berries blend best with butter.

Start to Finish:
10 minutes
Makes ¾ cup

½ cup butter or margarine,
    softened
½ cup thinly sliced
    strawberries
2 tablespoons powdered sugar

1. In a small mixing bowl combine butter or margarine, strawberries, and powdered sugar. Beat with an electric mixer on low speed until combined. Beat on medium speed until light and fluffy. Cover and refrigerate for up to 3 days. Serve at room temperature. Makes ¾ cup.

Nutrition Facts per teaspoon: 25 calories, 3 g total fat (2 g saturated fat), 7 mg cholesterol, 26 mg sodium, 0 g carbohydrates, 0 g fiber, 0 g protein
Daily Values: 2% vit. A, 1% vit. C, 0% calcium, 0% iron

Raspberry Butter

Start to Finish:
10 minutes
Makes ⅔ cup

½ cup butter or margarine,
    softened
3 tablespoons seedless
    raspberry preserves or
    other seedless fruit
    preserves
2 tablespoons powdered sugar

1. In a small mixing bowl beat butter or margarine, raspberry preserves, and powdered sugar with an electric mixer on medium speed until light and fluffy. Cover and refrigerate for up to 1 week. Serve at room temperature. Makes ⅔ cup.

Nutrition Facts per teaspoon: 32 calories, 3 g total fat (2 g saturated fat), 8 mg cholesterol, 29 mg sodium, 2 g carbohydrates, 0 g fiber, 0 g protein
Daily Values: 2% vit. A, 0% vit. C, 0% calcium, 0% iron

Cranberry-Orange Butter

Whole cranberry sauce adds color and texture to this zesty spread.

Start to Finish:
10 minutes
Makes 1 cup

½ cup butter or margarine, softened
⅓ cup canned whole cranberry sauce
2 tablespoons orange marmalade

1. In a small mixing bowl beat butter or margarine with an electric mixer on medium speed until light and fluffy. Add cranberry sauce and orange marmalade. Beat until well combined. Cover and refrigerate for up to 1 week. Serve at room temperature. Makes 1 cup.

Nutrition Facts per teaspoon: 22 calories, 2 g total fat (1 g saturated fat), 5 mg cholesterol, 20 mg sodium, 1 g carbohydrates, 0 g fiber, 0 g protein
Daily Values: 1% vit. A, 0% vit. C, 0% calcium, 0% iron

Maple Butter

Start to Finish:
5 minutes
Makes ¾ cup

½ cup butter or margarine, softened
¼ cup maple syrup or maple-flavored syrup

1. In a small mixing bowl beat butter or margarine and maple syrup with an electric mixer on medium speed until light and fluffy. Cover and refrigerate for up to 1 week. Serve at room temperature. Makes ¾ cup.

Nutrition Facts per teaspoon: 28 calories, 3 g total fat (2 g saturated fat), 7 mg cholesterol, 26 mg sodium, 1 g carbohydrates, 0 g fiber, 0 g protein
Daily Values: 2% vit. A, 0% vit. C, 0% calcium, 0% iron

Rum Butter

This sweet topping is similar to hard sauce—try it for dessert on Peach Pancakes (see recipe, page 28).

(see recipe, page 28)

Start to Finish:
10 minutes
Makes ¾ cup

½ cup butter or margarine, softened
3 tablespoons maple syrup or maple-flavored syrup
1 tablespoon powdered sugar
2 tablespoons dark rum

1. In a small mixing bowl beat butter or margarine, maple syrup, and powdered sugar with an electric mixer on medium speed until light and fluffy. Stir in rum. Cover and refrigerate for up to 1 week. Serve at room temperature. Makes ¾ cup.

Nutrition Facts per teaspoon: 34 calories, 3 g total fat (1 g saturated fat), 0 mg cholesterol, 30 mg sodium, 1 g carbohydrates, 0 g fiber, 0 g protein
Daily Values: 3% vit. A, 0% vit. C, 0% calcium, 0% iron

Herb Butter

Instead of sage and thyme, try basil and marjoram in this savory butter.

Start to Finish:
10 minutes
Makes ½ cup

½ cup butter or margarine, softened
2 teaspoons snipped fresh sage or ½ teaspoon ground sage
2 teaspoons snipped fresh thyme or ½ teaspoon dried thyme, crushed

1. In a small mixing bowl beat butter or margarine with an electric mixer on medium speed until light and fluffy. Add sage and thyme. Beat until combined. Cover and refrigerate for up to 1 week. Serve at room temperature. Makes ½ cup.

Nutrition Facts per teaspoon: 33 calories, 4 g total fat (2 g saturated fat), 10 mg cholesterol, 39 mg sodium, 0 g carbohydrates, 0 g fiber, 0 g protein
Daily Values: 3% vit. A, 0% vit. C, 0% calcium, 0% iron

Almond-Raisin Butter

Dried cranberries, dried blueberries, and dried tart red cherries all make excellent substitutes for the raisins.

Start to Finish:
10 minutes
Makes 1 cup

½ cup raisins
1½ teaspoons finely shredded
   orange peel (set aside)
2 tablespoons orange juice
2 tablespoons sliced almonds,
   toasted
½ cup butter or margarine,
   softened

1. In a blender container or food processor bowl, combine raisins and orange juice. Cover and blend or process with several on-off turns (do not grind). Add almonds; cover and blend or process with several on-off turns until chopped. Set aside.

2. In a medium mixing bowl beat butter or margarine and orange peel with an electric mixer on medium speed until light and fluffy. Add raisin mixture; stir until well combined. Cover and refrigerate for up to 1 week. Serve at room temperature. Makes 1 cup.

Nutrition Facts per teaspoon: 23 calories, 2 g total fat (1 g saturated fat),
5 mg cholesterol, 20 mg sodium, 1 g carbohydrates, 0 g fiber, 0 g protein
Daily Values: 1% vit. A, 0% vit. C, 0% calcium, 0% iron

Horseradish-Parsley Butter

Serve this pungent butter on Fresh Corn Pancakes (see recipe, page 36) or Shrimp and Spinach Pancakes (see recipe, page 54).

Start to Finish:
10 minutes
Makes ½ cup

½ cup butter or margarine,
   softened
2 teaspoons snipped
   fresh parsley
2 teaspoons horseradish
   mustard
1 teaspoon prepared
   horseradish

1. In a small mixing bowl beat butter or margarine with an electric mixer on medium speed until light and fluffy. Add parsley, mustard, and horseradish. Beat until combined. Cover and refrigerate for up to 1 week. Serve at room temperature. Makes ½ cup.

Nutrition Facts per teaspoon: 34 calories, 4 g total fat (2 g saturated fat),
10 mg cholesterol, 45 mg sodium, 0 g carbohydrates, 0 g fiber, 0 g protein
Daily Values: 3% vit. A, 0% vit. C, 0% calcium, 0% iron

Brandied Lemon Butter

Dress up plain crepes with this clarified butter.

Start to Finish:
10 minutes

Makes 1¾ cup

½ cup butter or margarine
1 cup sugar
4 teaspoons finely shredded
   lemon peel
½ cup lemon juice
⅓ cup brandy

1. To clarify butter, in a small heavy saucepan melt butter or margarine, without stirring, over low heat. When the butter is completely melted, there will be a clear, oily layer atop a milky layer. Slowly pour the clear, oily layer into a dish, leaving the milky layer in the bottom of the saucepan; discard the milky liquid.

2. Wash the saucepan. Return clarified butter to the saucepan. Add sugar, stirring until combined. Add lemon peel and lemon juice, stirring until sugar dissolves. Stir in brandy. Serve warm. Cover and refrigerate remaining butter for up to 1 week. Makes 1¾ cups.

Nutrition Facts per teaspoon: 21 calories, 1 g total fat (1 g saturated fat), 3 mg cholesterol, 11 mg sodium, 3 g carbohydrates, 0 g fiber, 0 g protein
Daily Values: 1% vit. A, 1% vit. C, 0% calcium, 0% iron

Caramel Apple Sauce

Make a snack of any sauce you have left. For example, serve it with graham crackers.

Start to Finish:
15 minutes
Makes 1¾ cups

1 tablespoon margarine
   or butter
1½ cups coarsely chopped,
   unpeeled apples
½ cup packed brown sugar
1 tablespoon cornstarch
⅔ cup half-and-half or
   light cream
2 tablespoons light-colored
   corn syrup
¼ cup coarsely chopped
   walnuts or pecans, toasted
½ teaspoon vanilla

1. In a heavy medium saucepan melt margarine or butter. Add apples; cook over medium heat about 2 minutes or until tender. Remove apple mixture from pan; set aside.

2. In the same saucepan combine brown sugar and cornstarch. Stir in half-and-half or light cream and corn syrup. Cook and stir until thickened and bubbly (mixture may appear curdled). Cook and stir for 2 minutes more. Remove from heat. Stir in apple mixture, nuts, and vanilla. Serve warm. Cover and refrigerate remaining sauce for up to 24 hours. Makes 1¾ cups.

Nutrition Facts per 2 tablespoons: 78 calories, 4 g total fat (1 g saturated fat), 4 mg cholesterol, 18 mg sodium, 12 g carbohydrates, 0 g fiber, 1 g protein
Daily Values: 2% vit. A, 1% vit. C, 1% calcium, 2% iron

Pancake Lore

Lumberjacks ate stacks of pancakes, but not by that name. Morning glories, sweat pads, string of flats, flat cars, slapjacks, simple stacks, and flannel cakes (suggesting the flannel shirts the loggers wore) all were lumber-camp lingo for pancakes.

Lemon Sauce

Gingerbread Pancakes (see recipe and photo, pages 12 and 13) are a natural match for this refreshing sauce.

Start to Finish:
15 minutes
Makes 1½ cups

Pancake Lore

*I*n the late 19th century, The Journal of American Folklore *reported that those who don't eat pancakes on Pancake Day won't have luck raising chickens or collecting their eggs.*

¾ cup sugar
5 teaspoons cornstarch
⅛ teaspoon ground nutmeg
1 cup water
1 tablespoon margarine
    or butter
1 teaspoon finely shredded
    lemon peel
3 tablespoons lemon juice
1 drop yellow food coloring
    (optional)

1. In a small saucepan stir together sugar, cornstarch, and nutmeg. Stir in water. Cook and stir over medium heat until thickened and bubbly. Cook and stir for 2 minutes more.

2. Remove from heat. Stir in margarine or butter, lemon peel, lemon juice, and, if desired, food coloring. Serve warm. Cover and refrigerate remaining sauce for up to 3 days. Makes 1½ cups.

Nutrition Facts per tablespoon: 31 calories, 0 g total fat (0 g saturated fat), 0 mg cholesterol, 6 mg sodium, 7 g carbohydrates, 0 g fiber, 0 g protein
Daily Values: 0% vit. A, 1% vit. C, 0% calcium, 0% iron

Hot Cranberry Sauce

This quick, tart sauce enhances Buckwheat Pancakes (see recipe, page 89).

Prep: 5 minutes
Cook: 10 minutes
Makes 2¼ cups

1 16-ounce can whole
   cranberry sauce
½ cup light pancake and
   waffle syrup
2 tablespoons margarine
   or butter

1. In a small saucepan combine cranberry sauce, syrup, and margarine or butter. Bring to boiling over medium heat. Reduce heat and simmer, uncovered, for 5 minutes, stirring occasionally. Serve warm. Cover and refrigerate remaining sauce for up to 1 week. Makes 2¼ cups.

Nutrition Facts per tablespoon: 31 calories, 1 g total fat (0 g saturated fat), 0 mg cholesterol, 13 mg sodium, 7 g carbohydrates, 0 g fiber, 0 g protein
Daily Values: 0% vit. A, 0% vit. C, 0% calcium, 0% iron

Pineapple Sauce

*Pair this sauce with Pineapple Pancakes (see recipe, page 35)
for a double pineapple treat.*

Start to Finish:
   10 minutes
Makes 2 cups

1 20-ounce can crushed
   pineapple (juice pack)
   Water
1 tablespoon cornstarch
1 tablespoon brown sugar

1. Drain the crushed pineapple, reserving the juice. Add enough water to the reserved pineapple juice to make 1⅓ cups.

2. In a medium saucepan combine cornstarch and brown sugar; stir in juice mixture. Cook and stir over medium heat until thickened and bubbly. Cook and stir 2 minutes more. Stir in pineapple; heat through. Serve warm. Cover and refrigerate remaining sauce for up to 1 week. Makes 2 cups.

Nutrition Facts per tablespoon: 15 calories, 0 g total fat (0 g saturated fat), 0 mg cholesterol, 1 mg sodium, 4 g carbohydrates, 0 g fiber, 0 g protein
Daily Values: 0% vit. A, 3% vit. C, 0% calcium, 0% iron

Spicy Apple Topping

Prep: 5 minutes
Cook: 20 minutes
Makes 1½ cups

With a flavor reminiscent of apple butter, this rich topping goes well on Apple Griddle Cakes (see recipe, page 29) or Honey-Oatmeal Pancakes (see recipe, page 11).

1 16-ounce can applesauce or
  2 cups chunky applesauce
¼ cup packed brown sugar
1 teaspoon lemon juice
½ teaspoon ground cinnamon
⅛ teaspoon ground nutmeg

1. In a medium saucepan combine applesauce, brown sugar, lemon juice, cinnamon, and nutmeg. Bring to boiling over medium heat. Reduce heat and simmer, uncovered, about 15 minutes or until it's the consistency of apple butter, stirring occasionally. Serve warm. Cover and refrigerate remaining topping for up to 1 week. Makes 1½ cups.

Nutrition Facts per tablespoon: 22 calories, 0 g total fat (0 g saturated fat), 0 mg cholesterol, 1 mg sodium, 6 g carbohydrates, 0 g fiber, 0 g protein
Daily Values: 0% vit. A, 0% vit. C, 0% calcium, 0% iron

Apricot Topping

Prep: 5 minutes
Cook: 10 minutes
Makes 2 cups

Serve this fruit-packed topping on Whole Wheat Griddle Cakes (see recipe, page 10).

1 15¼-ounce can unpeeled
  apricot halves
  Water
¼ cup packed brown sugar
2 teaspoons cornstarch
⅛ teaspoon salt
  Dash ground nutmeg
½ teaspoon finely shredded
  lemon peel
2 teaspoons lemon juice
½ cup pitted prunes, quartered

1. Drain apricot halves, reserving syrup. Add enough water to reserved syrup to equal 1 cup. Chop apricots; set aside.

2. In a medium saucepan combine brown sugar, cornstarch, salt, and nutmeg. Stir in reserved apricot syrup, lemon peel, and lemon juice. Cook and stir over medium heat until mixture is thickened and bubbly. Cook and stir for 2 minutes more. Stir in chopped apricots and prunes. Heat through. Serve warm. Cover and refrigerate remaining topping for up to 1 week. Makes 2 cups.

Nutrition Facts per ¼ cup: 86 calories, 0 g total fat (0 g saturated fat), 0 mg cholesterol, 38 mg sodium, 22 g carbohydrates, 2 g fiber, 1 g protein
Daily Values: 8% vit. A, 3% vit. C, 1% calcium, 4% iron

Peach and Banana Topping

Use leftovers of this topping drizzled over pound cake or angel food cake.

Start to Finish:
10 minutes
Makes 2 cups

1 8¼-ounce can sliced peaches
½ cup apricot or strawberry
    preserves
1 tablespoon margarine
    or butter
1 teaspoon lemon juice
1 medium banana, sliced
1 tablespoon brandy (optional)

1. Drain peaches, reserving juice. In a small saucepan combine apricot or strawberry preserves, margarine or butter, lemon juice, and enough reserved peach juice to make a slightly thickened sauce (1 to 2 tablespoons).

2. Bring mixture just to boiling over medium-high heat, stirring constantly. Reduce heat; stir in peach slices, banana slices, and, if desired, brandy; heat through. Serve warm. Cover and refrigerate remaining topping for up to 24 hours. Makes 2 cups.

Nutrition Facts per ¼ cup: 94 calories, 2 g total fat (0 g saturated fat), 0 mg cholesterol, 21 mg sodium, 21 g carbohydrates, 1 g fiber, 0 g protein
Daily Values: 3% vit. A, 5% vit. C, 0% calcium, 2% iron

Cherry and Pineapple Topping

Keep this almond-flavored topping in mind when you're serving Chocolate Fudge Pancakes (see recipe, page 65).

Start to Finish:
10 minutes
Makes 2 cups

1 21-ounce can cherry
    pie filling
1 8-ounce can pineapple
    tidbits, drained
¼ teaspoon almond extract
    Chopped almonds or pecans,
    toasted (optional)

1. In a small saucepan combine cherry pie filling, pineapple tidbits, and almond extract; heat through. Serve warm. If desired, sprinkle with almonds or pecans. Cover and refrigerate remaining topping for up to 1 week. Makes 2 cups.

Nutrition Facts per 2 tablespoons: 52 calories, 0 g total fat (0 g saturated fat), 0 mg cholesterol, 4 mg sodium, 13 g carbohydrates, 0 g fiber, 0 g protein
Daily Values: 0% vit. A, 3% vit. C, 0% calcium, 0% iron

Page numbers in bold italic indicate photographs.

A-E

Aebleskiver, Danish, 22, *23*
Almond-Raisin Butter, 103
Apples
  Apfelpfannkuchen (German Apple Pancake), 16, *17*
  Apple Griddle Cakes, 29
  Apple Topping, Spicy, 108
  Caramel Apple Sauce, 105
Apricot Topping, 108
Bananas
  Banana Pancakes, 33
  Peach and Banana Topping, 109
  Peanut Butter and Banana Fold-Overs, 75
Beet Pancakes, 38
Blintzes, Fruit, 25
Blueberries
  Blueberry Buttermilk Pancakes, 7
  Blueberry-Ricotta Pancakes, 26, *27*
  Blueberry Syrup, *27*, 94
Brie Pancake, 57
Brown Sugar Syrup, 97
Buckwheat
  Buckwheat and Pear Pancakes, 34
  Buckwheat Pancake Mix, 89
  Buckwheat Pancakes, *88*, 89
  Wheat Cake Wrap-Ups, 15
Buttermilk
  Basic Buttermilk Pancakes, 7
  Blueberry Buttermilk Pancakes, 7
  Buttermilk Pancake Mix, 80
  Buttermilk Pancakes, 81
  Cheese Buttermilk Pancakes, 7
Butters
  Almond-Raisin Butter, 103
  Brandied Lemon Butter, 104
  Cranberry-Orange Butter, 101
  Herb Butter, 102
  Horseradish-Parsley Butter, 103
  Maple Butter, 101
  Orange-Honey Butter, 99
  Raspberry Butter, 100
  Rum Butter, 102
  Spiced Honey Butter, 99
  Strawberry Butter, 100

Candy Bar Pancakes, Rolled, 70
Caramel Apple Sauce, 105
Carrot Cakes, 69
Cheese
  Blueberry-Ricotta Pancakes, 26, *27*
  Brie Pancake, 57
  Cheese Buttermilk Pancakes, 7
  Cheese Pancake Supreme, 62, *63*
  Cottage Cheese Crepes, Sweet, *66*, 67
  Cream Cheese Spread, 69
  Ham and Cheese Pancake Sandwiches, 50
  Ricotta-and-Spinach-Filled Crepes, 48, *49*
  Spinach and Cheese Pancakes, 45
Cherry and Pineapple Topping, 109
Chocolate
  Chocolate Chip-Peanut Butter Pancakes, 79
  Chocolate Fudge Pancakes, 65
  Chocolate Whipped Cream, 65
  French Silk Crepe Torte, 68
  Rocky Road Pancakes, 72, *73*
Cider and Maple Syrup, *9*, 95
Citrus Syrup, *83*, 98
Corn
  Corn Pancakes, Fresh, 36, *37*
  Potato and Corn Pancakes, 39
Cornmeal
  Cornmeal Pancake Mix, 82
  Orange-Cornmeal Pancakes, 82, *83*
Cranberries
  Cranberry-Orange Butter, 101
  Cranberry Pancakes, 32
  Cranberry Sauce, Hot, *88*, 107
  Cranberry Syrup, 96
  Nutty Cranberry Pancakes, 32
Cream Cheese Spread, 69
Crepes
  Basic Crepes, 61
  French Silk Crepe Torte, 68
  Mushroom-Filled Crepes, 56
  Ricotta-and-Spinach-Filled Crepes, 48, *49*
  Sweet Cottage Cheese Crepes, *66*, 67

F-L

Fruit. *See also* individual fruits
  Buckwheat and Pear Pancakes, 34
  Dried Fruit Pancakes, 28
  Fruit Blintzes, 25
  Tropical Fruit Pancakes, *30*, 31

Gingerbread Pancakes, *12*, 13
Grape Syrup, 96
Ham
  Ham and Cheese Pancake Sandwiches, 50
  Puff Pancake with Ham and Broccoli, *52*, 53
Herb Butter, 102
Honey
  Honey-Oatmeal Pancakes, 11
  Orange-Honey Butter, 99
  Raisin-Honey-Oatmeal Pancakes, 11
  Spiced Honey Butter, 99
Horseradish-Parsley Butter, 103
International
  Apfelpfannkuchen (German Apple Pancake), 16, *17*
  Danish Aebleskiver, 22, *23*
  Fruit Blintzes, 25
  Kaiserschmarrn (Emperor's Pancake), 24
  Palatchinken (Austrian Pancakes), 18
  Plättar (Swedish Pancakes), 19
  Sweet Hungarian Palacsinta, *20*, 21
Kid-pleasing
  Breakfast Tacos, 76, *77*
  Chocolate Chip-Peanut Butter Pancakes, 79
  Funny Face Pancakes, 74
  Peanut Butter and Banana Fold-Overs, 75
  Peanut Butter Pancakes, *78*, 79
  Rocky Road Pancakes, 72, *73*
  Silver Dollar Pancakes, 71
Lemons
  Lemon Butter, Brandied, 104
  Lemon Sauce, *12*, 106

M-R

Maple
  Cider and Maple Syrup, *9*, 95
  Maple Butter, 101
  Maple Syrup, Homemade, 94
Mixes
  Buckwheat Pancake Mix, 89
  Buttermilk Pancake Mix, 80
  Cornmeal Pancake Mix, 82
  Four-Grain Pancake Mix, 90
  Oatmeal Pancake Mix, 86
  Whole-Grain Pancake Mix, 92
  Whole Wheat Pancake Mix, 84

Mixes, pancakes made with
Breakfast Tacos, 76, **77**
Buckwheat and Pear Pancakes, 34
Buckwheat Pancakes, **88,** 89
Buttermilk Pancakes, 81
Candy Bar Pancakes, Rolled, 70
Carrot Cakes, 69
Corn Pancakes, Fresh, 36, **37**
Four-Grain Pancakes, 91
Funny Face Pancakes, 74
Oatmeal Pancakes, 87
Orange-Cornmeal Pancakes, 82, **83**
Oven Pancake, 51
Peanut Butter and Banana Fold-Overs, 75
Rocky Road Pancakes, 72, **73**
Tomato Pancakes, **46,** 47
Wheat Cake Wrap-Ups, 15
Whole-Grain Pancakes, 93
Whole Wheat Pancakes, 85
Mushroom-Filled Crepes, 56
Oatmeal
Honey-Oatmeal Pancakes, 11
Oatmeal Pancake Mix, 86
Oatmeal Pancakes, 87
Raisin-Honey-Oatmeal Pancakes, 11
Oranges
Orange-Cornmeal Pancakes, 82, **83**
Orange-Honey Butter, 99
Orange-Molasses Syrup, 97
Oven Pancake, 51
Palacsinta, Sweet Hungarian, **20,** 21
Palatchinken (Austrian Pancakes), 18
Pancakes à la Mode, 64
Peaches
Peach and Banana Topping, 109
Peach Pancakes, 28
Peanut Butter
Chocolate Chip-Peanut Butter Pancakes, 79
Peanut Butter and Banana Fold-Overs, 75
Peanut Butter Pancakes, **78,** 79
Peanut Butter Syrup, **78,** 98
Pineapple
Cherry and Pineapple Topping, 109
Pineapple Pancakes, 35
Pineapple Sauce, 107
Pizza on a Pancake, 51
Plättar (Swedish Pancakes), 19

Potatoes
Potato and Corn Pancakes, 39
Potato Pancakes, 40
Sweet Potato Pancakes, 41
Pumpkin Pancakes, 8, **9**
Raisin-Honey-Oatmeal Pancakes, 11
Raspberry Butter, 100
Rocky Road Pancakes, 72, **73**
Rum Butter, 102

S-Z

Sauces
Caramel Apple Sauce, 105
Chinese Sauce, 44
Cranberry Sauce, Hot, **88,** 107
Lemon Sauce, **12,** 106
Pineapple Sauce, 107
Sour Cream-Horseradish Sauce, 38
Tomato Sauce, Quick, 54
Shrimp and Spinach Pancakes, 54, **55**
Silver Dollar Pancakes, 71
Sourdough Pancakes, 14
Spinach
Ricotta-and-Spinach-Filled Crepes, 48, **49**
Shrimp and Spinach Pancakes, 54, **55**
Spinach and Cheese Pancakes, 45
Strawberry Butter, 100
Sweet Potato Pancakes, 41
Syrups
Blueberry Syrup, **27,** 94
Brown Sugar Syrup, 97
Cider and Maple Syrup, **9,** 95
Citrus Syrup, **83,** 98
Cranberry Syrup, 96
Grape Syrup, 96
Maple Syrup, Homemade, 94
Orange-Molasses Syrup, 97
Peanut Butter Syrup, **78,** 98
Spiced Syrup, 95
Tacos, Breakfast, 76, **77**
Tomatoes
Tomato Pancakes, **46,** 47
Tomato Sauce, Quick, 54
Toppings. *See also* Butters; Sauces; Syrups
Apple Topping, Spicy, 108
Apricot Topping, 108
Cherry and Pineapple Topping, 109
Chocolate Whipped Cream, 65

Toppings *(continued)*
Cream Cheese Spread, 69
Peach and Banana Topping, 109
Sweetened Whipped Cream, 62
Tropical Fruit Pancakes, **30,** 31
Vegetables. *See also* individual vegetables
Vegetable and Rice Pancakes, Crunchy, 44
Vegetable-Stuffed Puff Pancake, 60
Whole Wheat
Wheat Cake Wrap-Ups, 15
Whole-Grain Pancake Mix, 92
Whole-Grain Pancakes, 93
Whole Wheat Griddle Cakes, 10
Whole Wheat Pancake Mix, 84
Whole Wheat Pancakes, 85
Wild Rice Pancakes, **58,** 59
Zucchini Pancake, **42,** 43

Tips

bananas, using overripe, 33
batter, writing with, 74
buttermilk substitutes, 38
cast iron, seasoning, 22
cooking pancakes, 5
cream, whipping, 70
crepes, freezing, 61
eggs, choosing and using, 34
eggs, separating, 93
egg substitutes, using, 68
egg whites, beating to stiff peaks, 36
griddles, 5
margarine, using, 91
metric conversions, 112
mixes, measuring and storing, 80
mixing batter, 5
nonstick spray coating, using, 51
nutrition information, 8
nuts, toasting, 18
ovenproof skillets, 24
pancakes, freezing, 64
pancakes, keeping hot, 7
pancakes, making flavor variations, 92
prosciutto, buying and storing, 57
Sourdough Starter, replenishing, 14
sweet potatoes and yams, identifying, 41
syrup, warming, 97
wild rice, washing and cooking, 59

Cooking Hints for Metric Users

By making a few conversions, cooks in Australia, Canada, and the United Kingdom can use the recipes in *Better Homes and Gardens® Pancakes & Toppings* with confidence. The charts on this page provide a guide for converting measurements from the U.S. customary system, which is used throughout this book, to the imperial and metric systems. There also is a conversion table for oven temperatures to accommodate the differences in oven calibrations.

Product Differences: Most of the ingredients called for in the recipes in this book are available in English-speaking countries. However, some are known by different names. Here are some common American ingredients and their possible counterparts:
■ Sugar is granulated or castor sugar.
■ Powdered sugar is icing sugar.
■ All-purpose flour is plain household flour or white flour. When self-rising flour is used in place of all-purpose flour in a recipe that calls for leavening, omit the leavening agent (baking soda or baking powder) and salt.
■ Light corn syrup is golden syrup.
■ Cornstarch is cornflour.
■ Baking soda is bicarbonate of soda.
■ Vanilla is vanilla essence.
■ Green, red, or yellow sweet peppers are capsicums.
■ Golden raisins are sultanas.

Volume and Weight: Americans traditionally use cup measures for liquid and solid ingredients. The chart, *top right*, shows the approximate imperial and metric equivalents. If you are accustomed to weighing solid ingredients, the following approximate equivalents will be helpful.
■ 1 cup butter, castor sugar, or rice = 8 ounces = about 250 grams
■ 1 cup flour = 4 ounces = about 125 grams
■ 1 cup icing sugar = 5 ounces = about 150 grams
　Spoon measures are used for smaller amounts of ingredients. Although the size of the tablespoon varies slightly in different countries, for practical purposes and for recipes in this book, a straight substitution is all that's necessary.
　Measurements made using cups or spoons always should be level unless stated otherwise.

Equivalents: U.S. = Australia/U.K.

⅛ teaspoon = 0.5 ml
¼ teaspoon = 1 ml
½ teaspoon = 2 ml
1 teaspoon = 5 ml
1 tablespoon = 1 tablespoon
¼ cup = 2 tablespoons = 2 fluid ounces = 60 ml
⅓ cup = ¼ cup = 3 fluid ounces = 90 ml
½ cup = ⅓ cup = 4 fluid ounces = 120 ml

⅔ cup = ½ cup = 5 fluid ounces = 150 ml
¾ cup = ⅔ cup = 6 fluid ounces = 180 ml
1 cup = ¾ cup = 8 fluid ounces = 240 ml
1¼ cups = 1 cup
2 cups = 1 pint
1 quart = 1 litre
½ inch = 1.27 cm
1 inch = 2.54 cm

Baking Pan Sizes

American	Metric
8×1½-inch round	20×4-centimetre cake tin baking pan
9×1½-inch round	23×3.5-centimetre cake tin baking pan
11×7×1½-inch baking pan	28×18×4-centimetre baking tin
13×9×2-inch baking pan	30×20×3-centimetre baking tin
2-quart rectangular baking dish	30×20×3-centimetre baking tin
15½×10½×2-inch baking pan	30×25×2-centimetre baking tin (Swiss roll tin)
9-inch pie plate	22×4- or 23×4-centimetre pie plate
7- or 8-inch springform pan	18- or 20-centimetre springform or loose-bottom cake tin
9×5×3-inch loaf pan	23×13×7-centimetre or 2-pound narrow loaf tin or paté tin
1½-quart casserole	1.5-litre casserole
2-quart casserole	2-litre casserole

Oven Temperature Equivalents

Fahrenheit Setting	Celsius Setting*	Gas Setting
300°F	150°C	Gas Mark 2 (slow)
325°F	160°C	Gas Mark 3 (moderately slow)
350°F	180°C	Gas Mark 4 (moderate)
375°F	190°C	Gas Mark 5 (moderately hot)
400°F	200°C	Gas Mark 6 (hot)
425°F	220°C	Gas Mark 7
450°F	230°C	Gas Mark 8 (very hot)
Broil		Grill

Electric and gas ovens may be calibrated using Celsius. However, for an electric oven, increase the Celsius setting 10° to 20° when cooking above 160°C. For convection or forced-air ovens (gas or electric), lower the temperature setting 10°C when cooking at all heat levels.